Marketing and Trade of Forest Produce

Marketing and Trade of Forest Produce

Dr. Girish B. Shahapurmath
M.Sc. (Forestry) Ph.D.
Assistant Professor of Forest Management
Department of Natural Resource Management
College of Forestry, Sirsi (UK), Karnataka

Dr. S. S. Inamati
M.Sc. (Forestry) Ph.D.
Assistant Professor of Silviculture and Agroforesry
Department of Silviculture and Agroforestry
College of Forestry, Sirsi (UK), Karnataka

SSPH

SATISH SERIAL PUBLISHING HOUSE
403, Express Tower, Commercial Complex
Azadpur, Delhi-110033 (India)
Phone : 011-27672852, Fax : 91-11-27672046
e-mail : info@satishserial.com, hkjain1975@yahoo.com
Website : www.satishserial.com

Published by :

SATISH SERIAL PUBLISHING HOUSE

403, Express Tower, Commercial Complex, Azadpur, Delhi-110033 (INDIA)
Phone : 011-27672852 Fax : 91-11-27672046
E-mail : info@satishserial.com, hkjain1975@yahoo.com

ISBN 978-93-88020-67-1

Composed, Designed & Printed in India

About the Authors

Dr. GIRISH B. SHAHAPURMATH, M.Sc. (Forestry) Ph.D.
Assistant Professor of Forest Management
Department of Natural Resource Management
College of Forestry, Sirsi-581 401, Karnataka
University of Agricultural Sciences, Dharwad, India
E-mail: girishbshahapur@gmail.com /
shahapurmathgb@uasd.in

- Specialization in Silviculture and Agroforestry, Forest Management, Remote Sensing and GIS.
- Post Graduate Diploma in Agricultural Extension and Management (PGDAEM) by MANAGAE, Hyderabad during 2014-15.
- Post Graduate Diploma Computer Applications (PGDCA) by Infotech Computer Education and Manipal Institute of Computer Education (MICE) during 2008-09.
- Total 16 years of experience in the field of forestry (Teaching, Research and Extension).
- Presently working as Assistant Professor of Forest Management in Department of Natural Resource Management at College of Forestry, SIRSI (University of Agricultural Sciences, Dharwad, Karnataka (India).
- Recipient of "Outstanding Scientist Award" in Forestry by The Society of Tropical Agriculture, New Delhi, India in 7th International Conference on Agriculture, Horticulture and Plant Sciences held at Shimla (H. P.) during June 28-29, 2018.
- Recipient of "Best Teacher Award-2016" for outstanding contribution in the field of Forestry on the occasion of International Conference on "Rural Livelihood Improvement by Enhancing Farmers' Income through Sustainable Innovative Agri and Allied Enterprises (RLSIAAe)" organized by the Society for Upliftment of Rural Economy, Varanasi (India) during 30th October to 1st November, 2018 held at Birla Institute of Technology, Patna.
- Recognized as a Life Member for the "Society for Upliftment of Rural Economy, Varanasi (Membership No. LM/245/2018).
- First prize for Best Poster Presentation on Multistoreyed Cropping of Teak-perennial vegetables-legume based Agroforestry system

Presented in National Symposium (Silver Jubilee) on "Agroforestry Knowledge for Sustainability, Climate Moderation and Challenges Ahead" held at National Research Centre for Agroforestry, Jhansi (UP) from 15-17 December, 2008.

- First Prize for Best Poster presentation on "Forest Law and Models" presented in "National Kaanoonu Utsava" Exhibition held at Sirsi from 07.06.2014 to 06.07.2014 organized by Karnataka High Court, Bengaluru and District Law Service, Karwar and Bar Association, Sirsi.
- Worked as Principal Investigator and CO-Principal Investigator for 10 Research Projects.
- Field of interest - Silviculture and Agroforestry, Forest Management and Policy, Sustainable Forest Management, Remote Sensing and Geographical Information System in Forestry.
- Developed the course materials as reference books and for competitive exams, such as ASRB, IFS, ACF, RFO, KPSC, etc., in the field of forestry for students' purpose.
- Attended more than 15 Trainings/Summer/Winter schools, short courses, Seminars, Workshops, Conferences and undergone Agricultural Massive Open Online Courses (Ag MOOC).
- Published more 100 publications including Research papers in NAAS rated journal/Research notes/Papers presented and published in symposium/seminar/conference/workshop/Training/international conference/Popular articles published in journals/newspapers/ Books/chapters in books.

Dr. S.S. INAMATI, M.Sc. (Forestry) Ph.D.
Assistant Professor of Silviculture and Agroforestry
Department of Silviculture and Agroforestry
College of Forestry, SIRSI-581 401 Karnataka
University of Agricultural Sciences, Dharwad, India
E-mail: inamatiss@gmail.com/inamatiss@uasd.in

- Post Graduate Diploma in Rural Development (PGDRD) by IGNOU, New Delhi during 2004-05.
- Post Graduate Diploma Environmental Sustainable Development (PGDESD) by IGNOU, New Delhi during 2018-19.
- Worked as Subject Matter Specialist (Agroforestry), KVK, Gnagavati from 21.01.2006 to 04.11.2008
- Presently working as Assistant Professor of Silviculture and Agroforestry in the Deptt. of Silviculture and Agroforestry, College of Forestry, Sirsi Since 05.11.2008 till date (10 years)
- Total 15 years of experience in the field of forestry (Teaching, Research and Extension).
- Awarded "Best Presentation" in International conference on Agroforestry and Forestry Technologies, Amsterdam, The Netherlands in during January 20-22, 2018.
- Research areas of Interest - Site specific Silviculture, Forest tree nursery management, Vegetational studies, Forest modelling.
- Developed e-course materials and practical manuals for various courses of Silviculture and Agroforestry, Lecture Notes on Forest Mensuration, Lecture Notes Silviculture of Indian Trees, Lecture Notes on Quantitative Silviculture, Lecture Notes Productivity of Agroforestry systems.
- Attended more than 35 Conferences, Workshops, Trainings, Winter schools and short courses.
- Worked as Principal Investigator and CO-Principal Investigator for 12 Research Projects.
- Published more than 140 publications including Research papers in NAAS rated journal/Research notes/Papers presented and published in symposium/seminar/conference/workshop/Training/international conference/Popular articles published in journals/news papers/Books/chapters in books.

Hon'ble
Vice Chancellor

UNIVERSITY OF AGRICULTURAL SCIENCES, DHARWAD
KRISHI NAGAR, DHARWAD-581 005
KARNATAKA STATE, INDIA

Foreword

The forest products industry has vigorously opened up for global trade because the prevailing business model is built on capturing comparative advantages at the right cost. Many emerging countries possess valued forests, aspire for more processing industry and employment, and seek added value to their raw materials. International investors in the forest products industry are their willing allies but they want to ascertain predictable macroeconomic conditions, transparent fiscal incentives and abundant labour and preferably the rule of law and a sustainable wood supply to start with. A dynamic domestic market is now-a-days becoming an important factor in attracting foreign investments, and many emerging economies harbour bustling urban markets short of high-quality forest products.

Increasing trade in forest products has supported economic growth and eradication of poverty in a number of emerging countries. But trading out of poverty has proven difficult and it has led to further marginalization and events of misconduct in some countries. Safeguards must be firmly put in place to ensure that trade is based on legal and sustainable forest use, fair labour conditions and equitable sharing of benefits. Good governance is essential in setting the rules for sustainable production and trade.

FAO is supporting country efforts to develop the sustainable and legal trade of forest products. Producers in emerging countries gain improved access to quantitative and qualitative analyses on forest products trade and marketing issues including tariffs, impediments for market access and other trade restrictions.

Policy-makers and the private sector benefit from a wider coverage and a structured interpretation of forest products trade statistics and a higher degree of market transparency feeding into their forest decision making. Producers in emerging countries are better up-to-date on forest certification and legality verification, and understand more profoundly their implications for sustainable forest product trade, market access and product promotion. National and sub-national governments, local organizations, communities and other rights holders have the capacity to capture opportunities from forest carbon markets.

Producers in emerging countries know how to apply proven marketing strategies and practices in their local situations, including green marketing in the low-carbon economy, branding and ethical/fair trade tools, and enter into electronic marketplaces and social media networks.

More recently the forest sector has been entrusted with climate change mitigation targets of global importance. This has elevated forest issues higher on the political agenda than maybe ever before. Forest products embody and recycle large amounts of carbon, and trade moves products and their sinks around the world. This complex function will undoubtedly remain under a lively discourse in shaping the future role of forests in low-carbon economies and in the run-up to a global climate accord. Integrating concrete demands for carbon offsets in forests with the conservation of biodiversity and protection of watersheds, is a challenging equation in a world where consumption of forest products will continue to rise.

Textbooks on Marketing and Trade in Forestry suitable for undergraduate and post graduate students are very few particularly in Forestry Colleges in India. This textbook on "Marketing and Trade of Forest Produces" by Dr. Girish B. Shahapurmath and Dr. S. S. Inamati is a timely and welcome contribution in the forestry field. The authors have a considerable experience in teaching, research and extension in forestry/agroforestry and have presented the subject matter critically and systematically. This book will serve as a valuable source of information for the academicians in forestry institutes and also for the students for the preparation of competitive examinations in forestry discipline. I congratulate the authors for the hard work they put in, the systematic selection of topics and well documented and meticulous presentation.

I am hopeful that this text book will adequately meet the needs of students of forestry colleges and would be widely welcomed. I extend my best wishes to Dr. Girish B. Shahapurmath and Dr. S. S. Inamati for the success of their book.

May, 2019
Dharwad, Karnataka

Dr. M.B. CHETTI
(Vice Chancellor)
University of Agricultural Sciences, Dharwad
and Former Assistant Director General (HRD)
ICAR, New Delhi

Preface

Forestry, as a subject, is being taught to students of the Forest Colleges in different Agricultural Universities in India. This subject had been introduced as a subject for degree courses in most of the Indian Agricultural Universities. Indian Council of Agricultural Research (ICAR) provided an opportunity to start state-run forestry colleges in various State Agricultural Universities (SAUs) in the country. Earlier as per the recommendation of the National Commission on Agriculture, ICAR had started a course in 'Farm Forestry' during 1976 in all SAUs. There was a growing concern among the academicians and politicians alike that the students of forestry should have a greater exposure and access to natural forests. Increasing trade in forest products has supported economic growth and eradication of poverty in a number of emerging countries. But trading out of poverty has proven difficult and it has led to further marginalization and events of misconduct in some countries. Safeguards must be firmly put in place to ensure that trade is based on legal and sustainable forest use, fair labour conditions and equitable sharing of benefits. Good governance is essential in setting the rules for sustainable production and trade. Therefore, this book has been written to meet the requirements of the students of the Forest Colleges as well as those of the students preparing for competitive examinations.

The book covers mostly the present syllabi of the Forest Colleges as well as those of the competitive examinations (Indian Forest Service and State Forest Services). I claim no originality in writing this book except for the arrangement and presentation of the subject matter. A large number of books, journals and proceedings of symposia and workshops have been consulted. A list of these references is given at the end of book as references/bibliography.

I, therefore, gratefully acknowledge the help taken from "Agricultural Marketing in India" by S. S. Achraya and N. L. Agrawal., "Marketing and Trade of Forest Produce" by D. N. Tiwari and other publications mentioned in the references.

I am greatly indebted to Dean (Forestry) for constant guidance and help during the time of writing the book and improving it substantially. I am equally grateful to all the faculty members of College of Forestry, Sirsi (UAS, Dharwad, Karnataka) and officers of Karnataka Forest

Department for their valuable suggestions and help in writing the book as well as for reading through the chapters and making very valuable improvements.

Place: Sirsi, Karnataka
Date: 1st January, 2019

Dr. Girish B. Shahapurmath
Assistant Professor of Forest Management
Department of Natural Resource
Managment College of Forestry,
Sirsi (UAS, Dharwad)
Karnataka, India

Contents

Chapter 1

Nature and Scope of Marketing Approaches to Marketing and the Study of Marketing Functions with Special Reference to Forestry

Definitions and Meaning of Market

1. It is the place of region in which buyers and sellers exchange with one another.
2. Market is an area or place where buying and selling of various goods and commodities take place.
3. It is the place or building where commodities are brought or sold.
4. Market means a social institution which performs activities and provides facilities for exchanging commodities between buyers and sellers
5. *Kotler defined* market as an area for potential exchange.
6. Market is an area or place where buying and selling of various goods and services take place.

Definitions and Meaning of Marketing

1. Marketing is the business of buying and selling.
2. Marketing is the economic process by means of goods and services are exchanged and their values are determined in terms of the money.
3. According to *Kolter,* marketing is a human activity directed at satisfying the need and wants through exchange process.
4. American marketing association defines marketing as the performance of the business activity that direct the flow of goods and services from producer to consumer.

5. According to the national commission on agriculture, it is the process of and involves pre and post harvest operation, assembling, grading, storage, transportation and distribution.

Components of Market

1. Existence of goods and commodity
2. Existence of buyers and sellers
3. Business relationship between buyers and sellers
4. Demarcations of area such as place, region or country, etc.

Scope and Importance of Marketing

1. Producer Point of View

Market is a place where all producers can sell their produce. The producer looks at marketing from the point of view of price. Price may be guideline as to what type of crop to be grown, how much area to be covered and how much quantity should be brought to market for sale at once. From the producer point of view, it is important to know whether the prices prevailing in the market enable him to continue to produce or not, and what he should produce and where and at what time he should sell it. Large-scale production requires skill to sell it at remunerative price.

2. Consumers Point of View

Market is a place from where the consumer can get goods for daily requirements Marketing, therefore, renders services to the consumer in the sense of marketing goods, constantly available for meeting demands for consumer. The consumer, therefore, looks of marketing from the point of goods, their timely availability and the price at which they are offered. Marketing process brings new varieties, quality and beneficial goods to consumers. It provides connecting link between production and consumption.

3. Traders (middle man) Point of View

The traders' looks at marketing for keeping himself engaged in the business of buying and selling and thereby earning his livelihood. He gives selling and thereby he gives services to the society indirectly by making available goods and services needed for consumption. Middlemen try to increase his profit margin by discharging various marketing functions.

4. Government Point of View

In recent year government is paying more attention to the distribution of limited supply of Agricultural and Forestry output. The reduction in the output, coupled with continuance of high consumption in many areas, emphasizes the importance marketing mechanism as a means of keeping production and consumption in balance.

Scientific marketing also remedies the imbalance in the supply of making available the surpluses to the deficit areas. If the functions of marketing are not performed properly, the economic system may get out of balance resulting in piling up of goods with retailers, wholesalers and manufacturers, which lead to closure of factories and retrenchment of workers. Thus, it plays an important role in economic stability of a country.

5. Growth of Forest Based Industries

The forest marketing system helps in the growth of forest-based industries and stimulates the over all development process of the economy. Many industries depend on forestry for the supply of raw materials e.g. Paper industry, match industry, and plywood, handicrafts, etc.

6. Adoption and Spread of New Technology

The marketing system helps the farmers in the adoption of new scientific and technical knowledge. Marketing brings to the peasants useful implements, tools and fertilizers, etc. and the benefits of the use of machines and free after sales service, and make them modem farmers.

7. Addition to National Income

Marketing activities add to the nation's Gross National Product.

8. Employment

The marketing system provides employment to millions of persons engaged in various activities, such as packaging, transportation, storage and processing. Approximately one-third of all persons gainfully employed in the country are engaged in the field of marketing and about one-forth of National Income is earned by marketing profession.

9. Price Signals

An efficient marketing helps the farmers in planning their production in accordance with the need of the economy. This work is carried out through the price signals.

10. Optimization of Resource Use and Output Management

Forest Products marketing leads to the optimization of resource use and output management. An efficient marketing system can contribute to an increase in the marketable surplus by scaling down the losses arising out of the inefficient processing, storage and transportation. A well-designed system of marketing can effectively distribute the available stock of modern inputs and thereby sustain a faster rate of growth in the agricultural sector.

11. Increase in Farm Income

An efficient system guarantees to the farmers better prices for tree farm products and induce them to invest their surpluses in the purchase of modern inputs so that productivity may increase. This again results in increase in the marketed surplus and income of the farmers.

12. Widening of Markets

A well known marketing system widens market for products by taking them to remote corners of the country to areas far away from the production point e.g. teak produced in Maharashtra and Kerala are sold in another areas. The widening of the market helps in increasing the demand on a continuous basis and thereby guarantees a higher income to the producer.

13. Better Living

Any plan of economic development that aims at diminishing the poverty of forestry population, reducing consumer food prices, earning more foreign exchange or eliminating economic waste has to pay special attention to the development of an efficient marketing for food and forest products.

14. Creation of Utility

Marketing creates the following four types of utilities of the product :

i) **Place Utility :** The transportation function adds place utility to products by shifting them to a place of need from the place of plenty. Place utility added by the rate, road or water which transports the forest produce from one place to another place, where it can be consumed or stored. *e.g.* Transportation of logs from felling site to forest depot, transit depot or sell depot or processing unit, potatoes in plain areas, milk at urban places.

ii) **Possession Utility :** The marketing functions buying and selling helps in the transfer of ownership from one person to another in the marketing system. It is added to the forest product, when its ownership is transported to the final consumer or to someone in the marketing chain who is in a position to contribute other utilities to the product, as it passes from the production site to the ultimate consumer. Thus, all the processor or saw millers, stores or other handlers or forest depot or producer contribute possession utility.

iii) **Form Utility :** The processing function adds form utility by changing the raw material into finished products. *E.g.* Conversion of teak log into furniture, the fruits of *Garcinia indica* into Kokum (soft drink), Eucalyptus logs into pulp and paper; paddy into rice; Wheat into bread, biscuit, cake; Milk into ghee, cream, cheese, skimmed milk, butter, etc.

iv) **Time Utility :** The storage function adds time utility to the products by making them available at the time, when they are needed. *e.g.* Amla, tamarind, Rice in off-season, fish in cold storage etc.

v) **Service Utility :** The utility created by the rendering of some service not embodied in a material object, is known as service utility. All the personal services, which are rendered directly to the person of the consumer, create service utility. *e.g.* All public services which benefit citizens through the agency of the State, create utility (teacher, doctor, actor, etc).

vi) **Knowledge Utility :** The utility which is created through the impartation of knowledge is known as knowledge utility. *e.g.* Informative advertisement – One may not know the advantages of *Meswak* tooth paste manufactured by the extracts of the *Salvadora persica* plant. The brand was relatively unknown until a television advertising campaign during the 1998 Coca-Cola Cup spread brand awareness. So, an advertisement tells its attributes and advantages.

Approaches to the Study of Marketing

Marketing is a subject, which bristles with wide and varied problems. It includes the services and functions of different specialized institutions and middlemen. Different commodities have special marketing problems, therefore, the results of the study of one commodity may not be applicable to other commodity. Also, the same commodity will have different problems in different regions. Various approaches have been suggested and used to study marketing problems.

These are :

i) Functional approaches
ii) Institutional approaches
iii) Commodity approaches and
iv) Behavioural approaches

i) Functional Approach

A marketing function is an act, operation on service by which the original producer and the final consumer are linked producer and the final consumer are linked together. Marketing consists of many operations and an operation may be performed several times in the marketing process. The functional approach splits down the field of marketing into a few functions. This method analyses in detail the specific functions of marketing, such as buying, selling, transportation, storage, standardization, grading, financing, risk taking and marketing research.

The advantages of the functional approach in the study of agricultural marketing problems are:

1. We can make inter functional comparison of the marketing costs.
2. Inter agency comparison of the cost of performing a marketing function can be made.
3. Inter commodity comparison of cost of performing the various functions can also be made.

The defects of this approach are :

1. An undue emphasis on functions of marketing does not permit one to know how these functions are applied to specific business operations.
2. The marketing functions are so numerous that it is difficult to eliminate the unnecessary from the necessary functions.

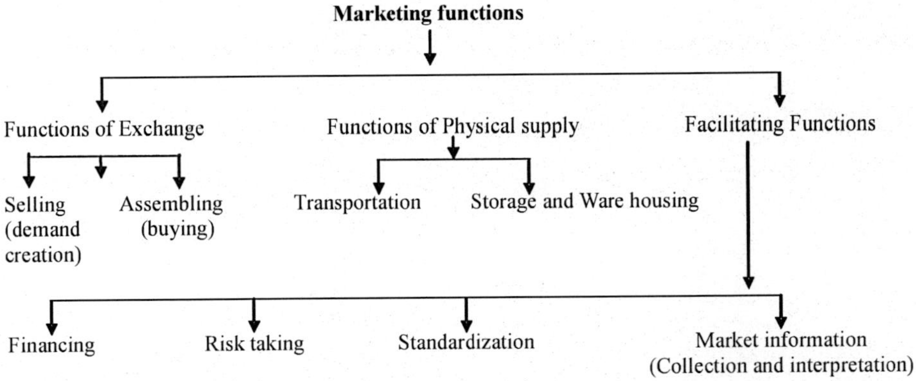

ii) Institutional Approach

The institutional approach to study of marketing problems implies a study of agencies and institutions, which perform various functions in the marketing process. The nature and character of various middlemen and other related agencies involved in the movement of the product are studied. The human element receives the primary emphasis. The agencies and institution, which perform various marketing functions are individuals, partnership, corporation, co-operatives, or government organizations.

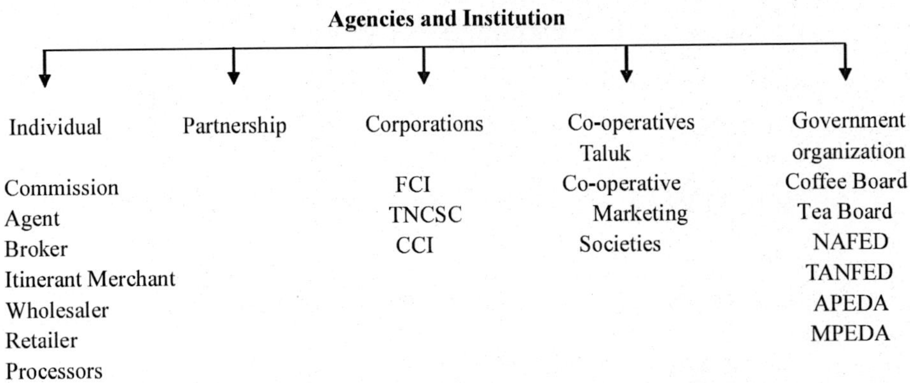

These agencies vary widely in size and ownership. They get their reward in the form of marketing margins. This approach helps us to find answers to the problems of 'who does what' in the marketing process, whether the margin of the agency is commensurate with the services rendered, which government regulations are necessary so that their unlawful activities may be curbed, and how to simplify the procedural system. The serious limitations of this method are that it leaves one with an inadequate understanding of marketing. Since the material presented is often largely descriptive and does not show effectively the inter-relations of the institutions studied.

iii) Commodity Approach

Under this approach, the commodity is the pivot around which all institutional and functional details are studied. The problems of marketing differ from commodity to commodity mainly because of the seasonality of production, the variations in its handling, storage, processing and the number of middlemen involved in them. For example, potatoes are stored in cold storage, while wheat is stored in godowns. Paddy, pulses and oilseeds are processed at miller's level. The main advantage of this approach is that it is concrete since all work relates to a specific product but it is a time consuming 'process and often results in excessive repetitions.

iv) Behavioural System Approach

This approach refers to the study of behaviour of firms, institutions and organizations, which exist in the marketing system for different commodities. The marketing process is continually changing in its organization and functional combinations. An understanding of the behaviour of the individuals is essential, if changes in the behaviour and functioning of the system are to be predicted.

Marketing Functions

Meaning

Any single activity performs in carrying a product from the point of the production to the ultimate consumer may be termed as marketing function. A marketing function may have any one or combination of three dimensions i.e. time, space and form. Marketing function involve in the movement of goods from the producer to its ultimate consumer vary from commodity, market to market, the level of economic condition of the country and final form of the consumption.

General Marketing Functions

1. Transportation
2. Packaging
3. Value addition
4. Processing
5. Storage
6. Advertisement

7. Electricity
8. Advise / consultancy
9. Communication - post
10. Labeling
11. Buying and Selling
12. Searching of consumer
13. Create demand
14. Distribution
15. Agency
16. Finance
17. Insurance
18. Stacking
19. Loading, unloading
20. Assembling
21. Quality control
22. Grading- standardization
23. Supervision
24. Account

Thomson Classification

1. Primary Functions
   1. Assembling
   2. Procurement
   3. Processing
2. Secondary Functions
   1. Packing
   2. Transportation
   3. Grading
   4. Quality control
   5. Storage
   6. Determination of price
   7. Risk taking
   8. Financing
   9. Buying and Selling
   10. Demand creation
   11. Dissemination of market information
3. Tertiary Functions
   1. Banking Insurance
   2. Communication post and telecommunication
   3. Supply of energy-electricity

Classification by Kahl's and Uhl

1. Physical Functions
   1. Storage and ware housing
   2. Grading
   3. Processing
   4. Transportation

2. Exchange Functions
    1. Buying
    2. Selling
3. Facilitative Function
    1. Standardization of grading
    2. Financing
    3. Dissemination of market information

Classification by Huegy and Mitchell

1. Physical Movement Functions
    1. Storage
    2. Packing
    3. Grading
    4. Transportation
    5. Distribution
2. Ownership Movement Functions
    1. Determining need
    2. Creating demand
    3. Finding buyers and seller
    4. Negotiation of price
    5. Rendering advice
    6. Transferring the title of goods
3. Market Management Functions
    1. Formulating policies
    2. Financing
    3. Providing organization
    4. Supervision
    5. Accounting
    6. Securing information

Marketing Functions (Kahl's and Uhl Classification)

Under the approaches to study of marketing, we have seen the marketing functions, marketing functions can be broadly classified as:

I. **Functions of exchange,** which includes selling and buying.

II. **Functions of physical supply**, which consist of transportation, storage and warehousing.

III. **Facilitating functions,** which comprise of financing, risk taking, standardization and market information.

I. Functions of Exchange

The process of passing goods into the consumer's hands is called function of exchange. It includes buying, assembling and selling.

Buying and Assembling

Buying is the first step in the process of marketing. Buying involves careful planning and needs setting up of policies and procedures. The following points are considered before a particular product is bought:

1. What to buy (Product)?
2. When and how much to buy? (Time and quantity)
3. From whom and where to buy? (Source)
4. On what terms and conditions and prices? (Price)

Assembling starts after the goods have already been purchased. It is a function separate from buying. Buying involves transfer of ownership of the goods, whereas assembling involves creating and maintaining of stock of goods purchased from different sources. The problems encountered in assembling of agricultural products are:

1. Seasonal production
2. Difficulties in controlling quantity and quality
3. Non- availability of information about sources of supply
4. Low quantity of marketable surplus.

Selling

The function of marketing is to ensure that the right product is made available at the right place, in the right quantity, at the right price, at the right time and under the right impressions to the consumer. All these righteousness is made possible by performing the sales function. Through selling function desires are created, hence it is called as **creative function.** Selling is also often referred to as **distribution function** because distribution makes good move from the place of production to the place of consumption. This is achieved through selling function.

Thus, buying, assembling and selling functions are directly concerned with change in the ownership of goods. They are complementary in nature. For every sale, there is a purchase and for every purchase there must be sale. And, assembling precedes a sale and assembling follows buying.

II. Functions of Physical Supply

Functions of physical supply/distribution includes determining warehouse locations (establishing a material handling system, maintaining an inventory control system, establishing procedures for processing orders) and selecting mode of transportation. Transportation and storage account for the major share in the total distribution cost.

Transportation

It is a necessary function of marketing because the most of the markets are geographically separated from the areas of production. It enhances the economic value through creation of place utility. The important function of transport is :

1. It helps in the growth of industries whose products require quick marketing e.g. vegetables, flowers, milk and fish.
2. It increases the demand for goods through widening of market
3. It creates place utility. As such transportation bridges the gap between production and consumption centres.
4. By virtue of improvement in the speed of transport, it offers time utility to products.
5. It helps in stabilization of prices by moving commodities from surplus area to deficit area.
6. Ensures even flow of goods into the hands of consumers.
7. It enables to consumers to enjoy the benefits of many goods not produced locally.
8. Transport intensifies competition, which, in turn, reduces prices. Prices are also reduced because of the facilities offered by transport for large-scale production.

Classification of transport

Broadly, various modes of transport fall under the three categories: Land, Water and Air. These are further classified on the basis of the vehicles used.

Road Transport

Merits : It is cheap, safe and flexible.

Demerits : It has got limited carrying capacity, slow speed, and unstable rates.

Rail Transport

Merits : Most suitable for heavy and bulky commodities. Long distance is quickly covered, cheap, all weather friend transport,

Demerits : Inflexibility, non-suitable for local transport and lesser accessibility.

Water Transport

Merits : Cheapest means of transport, high carrying capacity, creator of international trade and especially suitable for certain areas (forest products).

Demerits : Low speed, seasonal difficulties, longer journey required, international and political problems and limited area of operation.

Air transport

Merits : Rapid speed, no barriers and boon to perishable commodities.

Demerits : High rate, low carrying capacity, dependence on climatic conditions and high rate of accidents.

Storage and Warehousing

Storage is an important marketing function, which involves holding and preserving goods from the time they are produced until they are needed for consumption. While transportation is the process of transferring goods from one place to another, storage is a function, which helps in preserving goods in one place until they are needed at another place. Without storing transportation is impossible and storing is made possible by transportation.

Storage structures : a) Underground storage structures; b) Surface Storage Structures : Bag Storage Bulk or Loose Storage.

Warehousing : Warehouses are scientific storage structures specially constructed for the protection of quantity and quality of stored products. The important functions of the warehouse are:

1. Scientific storage
2. Financing
3. Price Stabilization
4. Market

Intelligence

Rural Godowns

The Government of India launched a scheme for the establishment of National Grid of Rural Godowns (NGRG) in July 1979. The scheme aims at the creation of network or rural godowns in the states and union territories, primarily to take care of the storage requirements of the small and marginal farmers. The scheme was launched with the following specific objectives.

Cold Storage

The term 'cold storage' refers to a refrigerated chamber for the storage of perishable commodities, such as fruits, vegetables, fish, eggs, meat, dairy products, etc. In a cold storage, the temperature is maintained in the range of 30 to 50° F. The other form of cold storage is freeze storage in which the temperature is kept below 30° F and the product remains at frozen state.

III. Facilitating Functions

Apart from function of exchange and function of physical supply, there is a third group of functions whose involvement in the process of marketing is rather indirect and remains as an undertone. Their importance and necessity cannot be ignored because they are helpful in minimizing various lags between production and consumption created by time, place, quantity and quality elements. These facilitating functions are financing, risk-bearing standardization and marketing information.

Financing

Between production and consumption ownership of commodities shifts many times, middlemen need finance not only for the purchase of stocks but also for performance of various marketing functions, such as processing, storage, packaging, transport and grading. The process of arranging necessary finance for marketing is termed as "Marketing Finance".

Risk bearing / Taking

Risk in marketing may be defined as uncertainty in regard to cost, loss, or damage. The risks associated with the marketing process are of three basic types :

1. **Physical Risk :** This includes a loss in the quantity and quality of the product during marketing process. It may be due to fire, flood, earthquake, insects, pests, fungus, excessive moisture or temperature, careless handling unscientific storage, improper packing, looting and arson.
2. **Price Risk :** Prices change not only year-to-year, but also during month-to-month, day-to-day or even on the same day.

Table : Value added as well as processing of by-products from agro raw materials.

Sl. No.	Commodity	Value added products		By-products processing
		Domestic market	Exports	
1.	Sugarcane	Sugar cubes	Sugar	Alcohol (industrial and portable from molasses, paper boards and paper from bagasse.
2.	Cotton	Yam and Textiles	Oil cake	Cotton seed oil (branded and refined), oil-cakes, cattle feed
3.	Fruits	Slices, juices, squashes, jams, jelly, fruit based drinks, pickles	Pulp, slices, juices, - squashes, jams, jelly, fruit based drinks and concentrates, pickles	-
4.	Spices	Processed and branded consumer pack, for the whole range of spices	Processed and branded consumer	-
5.	Other plantation crops	Tea and Coffee in and processed branded consumer branded silk materials packs,	Tea and coffee in processed and consumer packs, silk based products.	-
6.	Forest products	Paper, honey, bamboo based products, resins	Honey	Gum

Source: U.K. Srivastava and N. T. Patel, *Managing Food Processing Industries in India*, Oxford and **IBH** Publishing Co. Pvt. Ltd., pp. 18-19.

3. **Institutional Risk :** These include risks arising out of changes in government's budget policy, in tariffs and tax laws, in the movement restriction, statutory price controls, and the imposition of levies.

Processing

The term 'processing' may be defined a deliberate activity which changes the form of a commodity. It converts farm products into a more usable form. India's food processing involves only primary processing. It accounts for 80 per cent of the value. As much as 42 per cent of food industry is in the organized sector and 33 per cent in the small scale tiny and cottage sectors. In India, the agro-based industrialization has gained momentum during the last few years and the degree of processing has been intensified to get the higher value added products. Value added as well as processing of by-products from agro raw materials can be seen in the above Table.

Advantages of processing

1. It changes raw food into edible and palatable form
2. By processing, the value addition to farm products is increased e.g. Sugarcane into sugar, Wheat into flour, Mango into squash, pulp, pickles
3. Processing function makes it possible for us to store perishable and semi-perishable agricultural commodities for later use.
4. It generates employment
5. It widens market
6. Processing serves as adjunct to other marketing functions, such as transportation, storage and merchandising.

Standardization

It means the determination of the standards to be established for different commodities. Standards are fixed on the basis of certain characteristics, such as weight, size, colour appearance, texture, moisture content, amount of foreign matter present, etc.

Grading

Sorting of the unlike lots of the produce into different lots according to the quality specifications laid down. Grading follows standardization. It is a sub-function of standardization.

Advantages of grading

1. Grading before sale enable farmers to get a higher price for their produce.
2. Grading facilitates marketing
3. Grading widens market, without inspection, the sale can be effected over phone at distant places.
4. Grading helps consumers to get standard quality products at fair price shops.
5. Grading contributes to market competition and pricing efficiencies.

Grading helps the farmer :

- To get finance against pledging in CWC godowns
- To get claims settled by insurance companies and railways.
- Improve the keeping quality of stored products by removing inferior goods from the good lot.
- Facilitates future trading in a commodity.

Market information

Market information may be broadly defined as a communication or reception of knowledge or intelligence. It includes all the facts, figures, opinions and other information, which affect the marketing of goods and services. Market information is useful to all the sections of the society -Farmer, Producer, Middlemen, General Economy, and Government.

Market information is of two types

1. **Market Intelligence :** This includes information relating to such facts as the prices that prevailed in the past and market arrivals over time. It is historical nature. An analysis of the past helps to take decision about the future.
2. **Market News :** This term refers to current information about prices, arrival and changes in the market conditions. The availability of market news in time and with speed is of utmost value.

- **Marketing Research :** It is defined as gathering, recording and analyzing of all facts about problems relating to the transfer and sale of goods and services from producer to consumer.
- **Market Research :** It describes research on markets, their size, geographical distribution, and incomes and so on. It is a sub-function of marketing research.

Methods of Quality Control

The quality control can be effected at the time of production itself for manufactured goods, but it is not so for agricultural produce because agriculture production is done in harmony with nature. Farmer has little or no control over nature.

The possible source of quality deterioration during production are pest and disease attack, weed, seed mixing, non filling of grains due to late flowering, mixture and off types and other varieties, inclusion of foreign matter. These quality-deteriorating factors can be reduced at the time of harvest and cleaning. And also, grading can be done to get better price for quality produce. But the grading at producers level is not popular in India.

During processing the traders in order to make quick profit may deliberately include foreign matter like stone, things imitating produce, mixing old produce with current year harvested produce some of there materials may also cause injury to human health. The 'agmark' laboratories do the quality control at consumer level. But it is only voluntary. If the consumers are quality conscious and demand the quality produce, the marketing middlemen cannot but provide the quality produce. Even some private traders to create a separate market share for their produce enforce quality tests. Since India is poor country the 'agmark' labelling cannot be made compulsory. Through improvement in literacy, by conducting quality awareness programmes during exhibitions and propagating through mass media quality in agricultural produce can be enforced.

❑❑❑

Chapter 2

Dimensions and Classification of Markets

Dimensions of a Market

There are various dimensions of any specialized market. These dimensions are:

1. Location or place of operation
2. Area or coverage
3. Time span
4. Volume of transactions
5. Nature of transactions
6. Number of commodities
7. Degree of competition
8. Nature of commodities
9. Stage of marketing
10. Extent of public intervention
11. Type of population served
12. Accrual of marketing Margins

Classification of Market

Marketing may classified on the basis of the following dimensions:

I. On the Basis of Location or Place of Operation

1. Village Market

These markets are located in a small village where smaller transaction takes place among buyers and sellers of a village. *e.g.* Farmer - Village traders.

2. Primary Market

These markets are located in town near the centre of production. In this market major part of the produce is brought for selling transaction usually between farmer and primary traders. *e.g.* TSS market, Sirsi, NTFP market, Siddapur.

3. Secondary Wholesale Market

These markets are located at district headquarter or at important trade centre, where major transaction takes place between village traders and wholesalers.

4. Terminal Market

This is a market point from which produce directly dispose off to consumer or processor or assemble for export which is called as terminal market. In this market merchants are well-organized and use modern method of marketing. These markets are always located in Metro cities like Delhi, Mumbai, Chennai, Kolkata, etc.

5. Sea Board Market

These are located near seashore and mainly for import and export of goods. e.g. Mumbai, Chennai, Kolkata, Cochin, etc.

II. On the basis of Area or Coverage

1. Local Market

This is a market where the buying and selling activities are confirmed among the buyers and sellers drawn from same village or nearby village. The village market exists mostly for perishable commodities in a small lot. e.g. - Fish Market, local milk market, vegetable market, etc.

2. Regional Market

This is a market where buyers and sellers for a commodity are drawn from a larger area than local market. This market usually exists for food grain.

3. National Market

This is a market where the buyers and sellers spread at National level. e.g. Jute market at Kolkata, Resin market in Uttaranchal, tea market in Assam.

4. World or International Market

This is a market where the buyers and sellers are drawn from more than one country or world. These are the biggest markets from the area point of view.

III. On the basis of Time Span

1. Short Period Market

The markets prevailing only for a day or few hours are called short period market. The product in this market is perishable in nature. e.g. fish, vegetable, meat, etc.

In Black market, scare commodities are sold at a very high price but not openly in a secrete manner. The situation arises on account of excess of demand over limited supply. So, Black market is anti-social activity which gives to reed to black money which is also known as invisible market.

2. Periodic Market

In this market, buyers and sellers comes together at specific space at specific time and day in a village or in semi-urban areas. It is generally held weekly, biweekly, fortnightly and monthly.

3. Long Period Market

This market prevails for a longer period and commodities are less perishable for some-time. e. g. food grain, oil seeds.

4. Secular Market

These are the permanent and well established markets, where durable commodities can be sold for many years.

IV. On the Basis of Volume of Transaction

1. Wholesale Market

In this market, commodities are brought and sold in large lots or in bulk. It is generally located in towns and cities. Retailers purchase goods from wholesale market at a reasonable rate. ***Mashakhores*:** This is a local term used for big retailers or small wholesalers dealing in fruits and vegetables. Earlier, the *mashakhores* used to deal only in one.

2. Retail Market

A retail market is one in which commodities are brought and sold to the consumer as per their requirement. Transaction in this market takes place between retailer and consumer. This market is very near to consumer. Transaction quantity is generally smaller than that in wholesale market.

V. Nature of Transaction

1. **Spot on Cash Market :** A market in which goods are exchanged for money immediately after sale.
2. **Forward Market :** A market in which purchase and sale takes place at time and exchange of commodities takes place on some specified date.

VI. On the Basis of Number of Commodities in which Transaction Takes Place

1. General Market

A market in which all types of commodities, such as food grains, oil seeds, fibers, medicinal plants, timbers are brought and sold is known as general market.

2. Specialized Market

In this market selling and buying takes place for specialized produce.

VII. On the Basis of Degree of Competition

On the basis of competition, markets may be classified into the following categories :

a) Perfect Markets

A perfect market is one in which the following conditions holds good :

1. There are a large number of buyers and sellers.
2. All the buyers and sellers in the market have perfect knowledge of demand, supply and prices.
3. Prices at any one time are uniform over a geographical area, plus or minus the cost of getting supplies from surplus to deficit areas.

4. The prices are uniform at anyone place, over periods of time, plus or minus the cost of storage from one period to another.
5. The prices of different forms of a product are uniform plus or minus the cost of converting the product from one form to another.

b) Imperfect Markets

The markets in which the conditions of perfect competition lacking are characterized as imperfect markets. The following situations, each based on the degree of imperfect, may be identified :

i) ***Monopoly Market :*** Monopoly is a market situation in which there is only one seller of a commodity. He exercises sole control over the quantity or price of the commodity. e.g. Railways.

ii) ***Duopoly Market :*** A duopoly market is one, which has only two sellers of a commodity, e.g. two retailers in a village.

iii) ***Oligopoly Market*** : A market in which there are more than two but still a few sellers of a commodity is termed as an oligopoly market e.g. different air lines operating in our country.

iv) ***Monopolistic Competition :*** When a large number of sellers deal in heterogeneous and differentiated *form* of a commodity, the situation is called monopolistic competition. e.g. Tea and Coffee by different companies, pump sets, fertilizers, etc.

VIII. On the Basis of Nature of Commodity

1. Commodity Market

Market which deals with the goods and raw materials, such as plywood, furniture, timber, bamboo and other minor forest produce is known as commodity market.

2. Capital Market

This market is related with shares and bonds. e. g. Money market, Share market.

IX. On the Basis of Stage of Marketing

1. Producing Market

This market mainly assembles the commodity for further distribution to other market. It is termed as producing market. It is always located in producing areas.

2. Consuming Market

Market which collect the produce for final distribution to consuming population are called consuming market.

X. On the Basis of Extent of Public Intervention

1. Regular Market

These are the markets in which business is done in accordance with the rules and regulation framed by the organization.

2. Unregulated Market

These are the markets in which business is conducted without any set of rules and regulations.

XI. On the Basis of Type of Population Served

1. Urban Market

It is situated in urban areas to fulfill the requirement of urban people.

2. Rural Market

It is situated in rural areas to fulfill the requirement of rural peoples.

XII. On the Basis of Market Functionaries

1. Farmer Market
2. Co-operative Market
3. General Market

Characteristics of Agricultural, Horticultural and Forest Produce

The special characteristics, which the agricultural, horticultural and forest produce possess, make them differ from the manufactured products marketing :

1. ***Perishability of produce*** : Most of the farm produce is perishable in nature, but the period of perishability varies from few hours (flowers) to a few months (grains). The extent of perishability of the farm produce may be reduced by the processing function (chilling of milk) but they cannot be made non-perishable like manufactured products.
2. ***Seasonality of production*** : Traditional varieties are season bound in production but the high yielding varieties are not that much season bound but even then the availability of water facilities, temperature, wind, solar radiation to dry the produce make major part of agricultural production in particular season.
3. ***Bulkiness of products*** : The bulky characteristic of most of farm products makes their transportation and storage difficult and expensive. These increase the price spread.
4. ***Variation in quality of produce*** : Compared to manufacture goods there is large variation in the quality of agricultural products, which make their grading, and standardization somewhat difficult.
5. ***Irregular supply of agricultural products*** : The supply of agricultural products is uncertain and irregular because of the dependence of agricultural production on natural conditions. With the varying supply, the demand remaining almost constant, the price of agricultural produce fluctuate substantially.
6. ***Small size of holdings*** : Farm products are produced throughout the length and breadth of the country and most of the producer's holdings are small in size. This makes the estimation of supply difficult and creates problem in marketing.
7. ***Processing*** : Most of the farm products have to be processed before their consumption by ultimate consumers. The processing function increases the price spread of agricultural commodities. The processing firms enjoy the advantage of monopsony, duopsony or oligopsony in the market. This situation creates disincentives for the produces and may have an adverse effect on production in the next year.

❑❑❑

Chapter 3

Market Structure and Dynamics of Important Timber and Non-timber Markets

Meaning of Market Structure

Market Structure refers to the size and design of market :

i) Market Structure refers to those organizational characteristics of market which influence the nature of competition and pricing and affect the conduct of business of firm.

ii) It is the characteristic of market which affect traders' behaviour and their performance.

iii) Market structure is a formal organization of the functional activities of a marketing institution.

Components of Market Structure

Components of a Market Structure, which together determine the conduct and performance of the market are:

1. Concentration of market power,
2. Degree of product differentiation,
3. Conditions of entry of firms in the market
4. Flow of market information and
5. Degree of integration.

1. Concentration of Market Power

It is an important element determining the nature of competition and consequently of market conduct and performance. This is measured by the no. and size of firms existing in market. The extent of concentration represents the control of an individual firm or group of firm over the buying and selling of produce. A high degree of market concentration restricts the movement of goods between buyers and sellers at fair and competitive price and thereby creates an oligopoly situation in the market.

2. Degree of Product Differentiation

Whether or not the products are homogeneous, affects the market structure. If products are homogenous, the price variation in market will not be wide. When products are heterogeneous, firms have the tendency to charge different prices for their product. Everyone tries to prove that his product is superior to product to others.

3. Condition for Entry of Firm in the Market

Another dimension of market structure is the restrictions, if any, on the entry of firm in the market. Sometimes, a few big firms do not allow new firms to enter the market or make their entry difficult by their dominance in the market. There may also be some government restrictions on the entry of the firms.

4. Flow of Market Information

A well-organized market intelligence, information system helps all the buyers and sellers to freely interact with one another in arriving at prices and striking deals.

5. Degree of Integration

The behaviour of an integrated market will be different from that of a market, where there is no or less integration either among the firms or of their activities. Firms plan their strategies in respect of the methods to be employed in determining prices, increasing sales, coordinating with competing firms and adopting predatory practices against rivals or potential entrants. The structural characteristics of the market govern the behaviour of the firms in planning strategies for their selling and buying operations.

Dynamics of Market Structure (conduct and performance)

The market structure determines the market conduct and performance. The term **Market Conduct** refers to the patterns of behavior of firms, especially in relation to pricing and their practices in adopting and adjusting to the market in which they function. Market conduct includes :

1. Market sharing and Price setting policies
2. Polices aimed at coercing rivals and
3. Policies towards specification of the quality of products.

The term **Market performance** refers to the economic results that flow from the industry, as each firm pursues its particular line of conduct.

Some of the criteria for measuring market performance and of the efficiency of the market structure are :

1. Efficiency in the use of resources, including real cost of performing various marketing functions.
2. The existence of monopoly or monopoly profits, including the relationship of margins with the average cost of performing various functions.
3. Dynamic progressiveness of the system in adjusting the size and number of firms in relation to the volume of business in adopting technological innovations and in finding and / or inventing new forms of products so as to maximize general social welfare.
4. Whether or not the system aggravates the problem of inequalities in inter-personal, inter-regional or inter group incomes.

For a satisfactory market performance, the market structure should keep pace with the following changes :

a) Production pattern

b) Demand pattern

c) Costs and patterns of marketing functions

d) Technological change in industry

□□□

Chapter 4

Marketing Channels, Costs, Marketing Margins and Price Spread - Concepts and Applications

Marketing Channel

Meaning

Marketing channels are routes through which forest produce or products move from producer/collector/cultivator to consumer. The path or route, followed by the commodity which collect the produce to final consumer is known as marketing channel. The length of channels varies from commodity to commodity, depending on the quantity to be moved, form of consumer demand and degree of regional specialization in production. The chain of intermediaries through whom the various food products pass from producers to consumers constitute the marketing channel. The length of the channel varies from commodity to commodity depending upon the quantity to be moved, the form of consumer demand and degree of regional specialization in production.

Rice marketing channel

Producer (Paddy) → Wholesaler → Rice miller → Rice → Wholesaler → Retailer → Consumer

Producer → Procurement centers → Civil supply modern rice mill → Fair Price Shop → Consumer

Types of Channels

1. Direct Channel

There are no middlemen. Goods are transferred directly from producer to consumer. There is complete absence of middleman or intermediaries. The quantity of transaction is very less.

2. Indirect Channel

There is one or more than one middle man in distribution of goods linking producer and consumer. The forest commodities generally move from producer to consumer through intermediaries or middlemen.

Middleman

The forest produce passes through the large number of middlemen until it reaches the final consumer. Middleman is an independent businessman situated in marketing channel at a point between producer and consumer and he is specialized in performing the various marketing functions and rendering such services which are involved in the marketing of goods. There are several intermediates comprises of village traders, agent, contractor, transporter, etc. The functions of various stages in this process are assembling and distribution of product. The existence of long chain of middlemen reduces the share of the consumer price received by the actual cultivars.

Types of Middleman

Merchant Middleman

He buys small quantity of the product from the producer and resells to village trader, wholesaler, retailer, village merchants, etc. They buy and sell on their own with gain or loss, depending on the difference in the sale and purchase prices.

Agent Middleman

Agent middleman is the representative of the clients and he negotiates a purchase or sale or both but not take goods in which he deals. They don't take any quantity of the produce and therefore, don't own it. The merchants always buy and resale, whereas agent is not involved in buying and selling transaction. They receive income in the form of commission or brokerage. *e.g* : Broker, commission agent manufacturer agent, auctioneer, packing and forwarding agent, warehouseman, export-import agent, other functionaries, government procurement agencies.

Speculative Middleman

They are not regular buyers or sellers. They are specialized in risk taking. They buy at low price and sell in the off-season, when price are high.

Processor

Processor carries on their business either on their business own or on custom basis. They also engage in advertising activity to create a demand for their processed products.

Facilitative Middleman

Some middlemen don't buy and sell directly but assist in the marketing process. They receive their income in the form of fees or service charges from those who utilize their services. e.g. hamals, graders, transport agency, communication agency, advertising agency, auctioneers, etc.

Primary Suppliers

Most of the timber species available in the wood markets are obtained from the lands of the farmers. The tree crops raised on the community lands is sold through auctions. Wood from forests and plantations on government lands are auctioned by the forest department.

Intermediary Buyers/Users

Contractors purchase trees from farmers, as they find it difficult to arrange for the harvest and transportation of trees harvested. The contractors charge about 5% of their market price of the produce. Sometimes farmers loose heavily as contractors make an under assessment of the tree crop of the farmer. Commission agents/timber merchants arrange the sale of wood in the market on behalf of the either the farmers or the contractors and charge 4-5% of the commission. In saw mills, the logs of timber are into suitable size and shapes as per the requirement of various users. Veneer/peeling units purchase logs and after peeling them into veneers and supply to the plywood/plyboard industries.

Secondary Buyers/ End users

Plyboard Industries either have their own peeling units or purchase veneers from the peeling units. Saw mills manufacture wooden boxes and crates of eucalyptus for packing and storage of food grains and fruits. FCI and fruit traders purchase wooden crates and boxes. The wooden construction material of eucalyptus and other timber species are mostly supplied to the building constructors by the timber merchants and saw mills. In brick kilns also, eucalyptus wood is used as firewood in a limited way. The paper industry at Ballarpur use bamboo on a large scale and subabhul on small scale. Apart from eucalyptus, bamboo, subabhul, veneer waste and saw mill waste are also bought by the paper mills.

Leakages in Marketing System

Commission agents and contractors are the two intermediaries between farmers and end users who do not contribute to the value addition of the wood and yet they play major role in marketing system. Since they do not contribute in the value addition of the wood, their presence in the system result in heavy leakage in the profit margins of the farmers.

The marketing channels for commercially extracted and marketed forest produced in Konkan region.

Marketing Channels for Bamboo

Farmer / Bamboo Grower ↘ Handicraft man
↓
Village merchant
↓
Wholesaler
↙ ↓ ↘
Consumer Distant market (Mumbai, Banglore, Miraj, Sangli, Nasik)
↓
Building contractors

Marketing Channels of Teak

Producer / Farmer / Teak grower

↓

Village merchant

↓

Wholesaler

↓

Distant market

↓

Building contractor

↓

Consumer

Marketing chain

The timber industry consists of a chain of successive manufacturing activities, each having traded outputs. Each part of the chain absorbs some of its added value. The figure below provides an overview of raw material and wood product flows in the forest processing industry. Primary processing includes the transformation of logs into primary timber products, such as sawnwood, veneer and plywood. Further processing here refers to the manufacture of higher value added products, such as joinery and furniture.

The wood processing industry

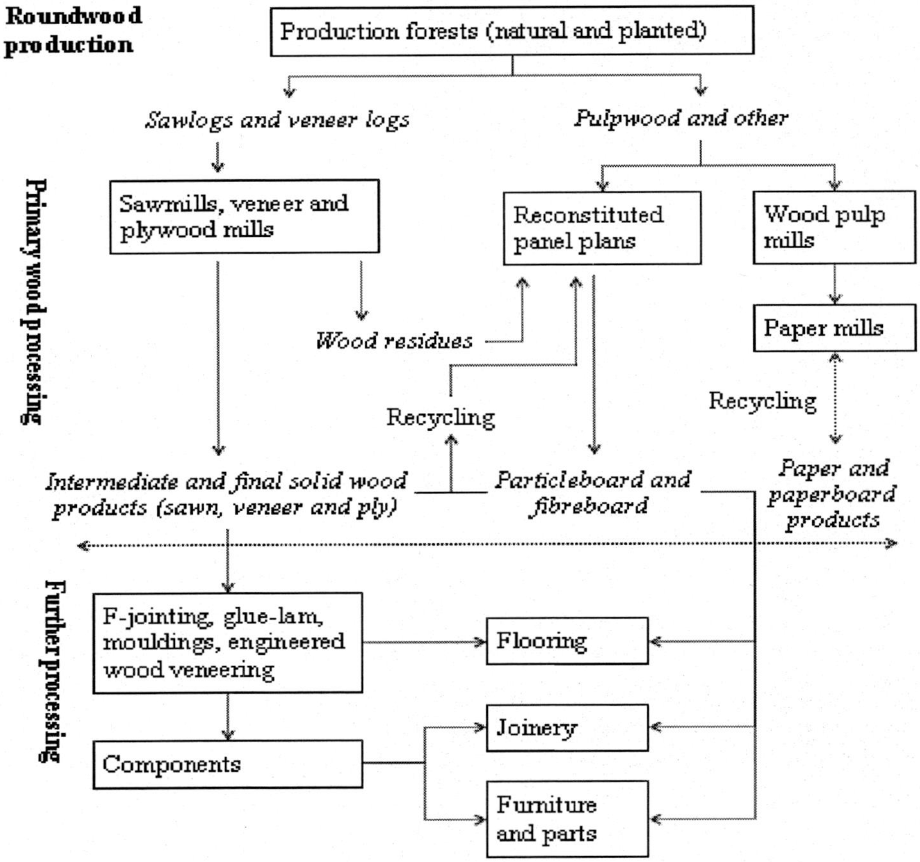

Source: Adapted from International Trade Centre/International Tropical Timber Organization. *Tropical Timber Products: Development of Further Processing in ITTO Producer Countries*. Geneva: ITC/ITTO, 2002.

There are normally several layers between timber producers and end users. The figure below gives a schematic overview of the international trade channels for tropical plywood.

Trade channels, tropical plywood

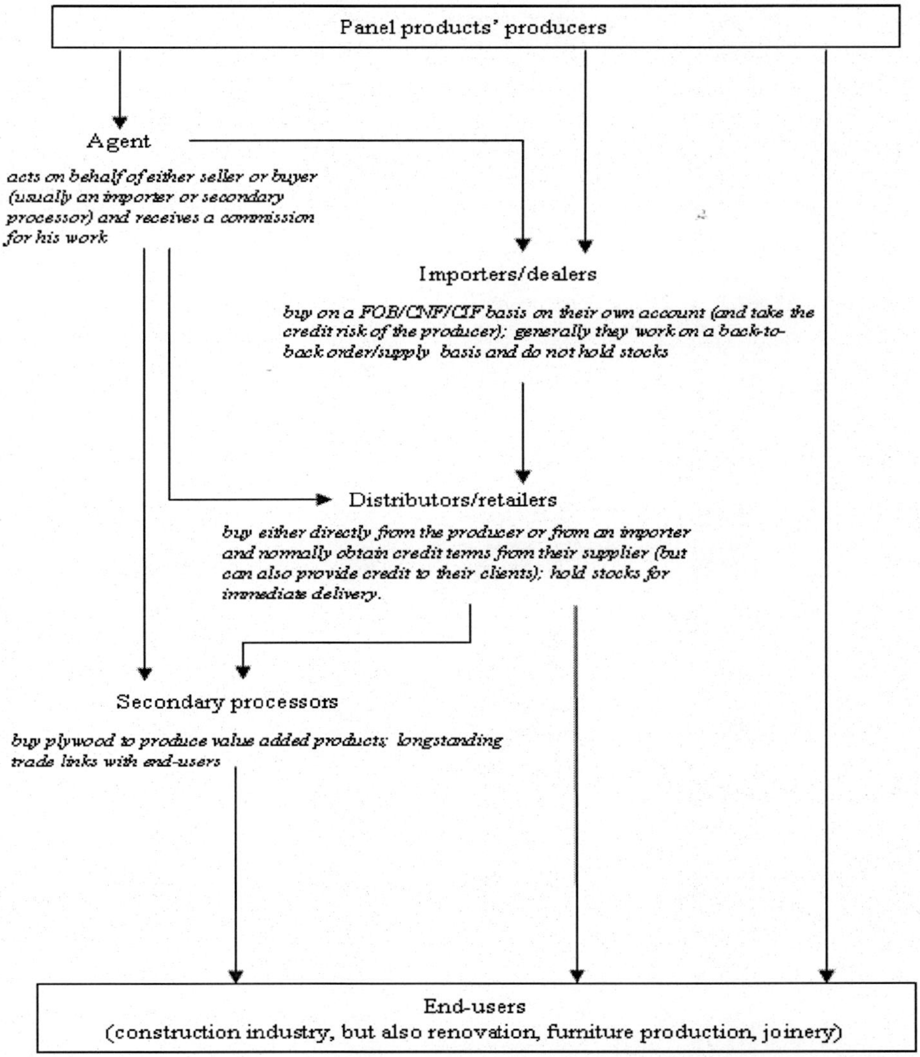

Source: Adapted from L. Rutten and S.H. Tan. *Reviving Tropical Plywood*. ITTO Technical Series No. 20. Yokohama, Japan: ITTO, 2004.

The most common trade channels in international plywood trade are:

- Direct contract sales to overseas customers, often through sales offices or agents;
- Sales to traders, pre-dominantly based in Singapore and Hong Kong, China; and

- Sales to representatives of overseas companies, who are buying directly at origin.

Direct contract sales to overseas customers, often through sales offices or agents, is the common form of trade for sales to Europe. Apkindo, the Indonesian Plywood Association, used to have sales offices in China, Japan and the Middle East. Malaysian firms also have overseas representative offices, where they do not have offices, they sell through agents.

Most Indonesian exporters sell to the Middle East through Singapore traders. Sometimes, they sell through Japanese trading houses for their sales to the United States and through traders based in Hong Kong, China for sales to mainland China. Several Japanese trading houses now have buying offices in Indonesia, whereas previously they had bought from Apkindo's Nippindo office in Japan.

An important development within the timber industry is the shortening of the supply chain. Some end-users, such as large construction firms and large furniture manufacturers in Japan and Europe, are making an effort to bypass the traditional importing firms.

Marketing Cost, Market Margin and Price Spread for Different Forest Produce

Meaning of Marketing Cost

Marketing cost are the actual expenses required for bringing goods and services from producer to consumer. Accordingly cost in case of forest crop begins, when they leave the forest area and end at the point where they finally reach the consumer.

The cost involved in moving the product from the point of production to the point of consumption i.e. the cost of performing the various marketing functions and of operating various agencies is called **marketing cost.**

The market functionaries involved in moving the produce from the initial point of production till it reaches the ultimate consumer, charge profit margin for the service rendered.

The cost involved in marketing plus the profit margin charged by the market functionaries for the service rendered constitute **market margin**.

Constituents of the Marketing Cost

- Handling charges at local point
- Assembling charges
- Transportation and storage cost
- Handling charges by middleman
- Expenses on secondary services, financing, risk taking and market intelligence
- Profit margin taken out by various agents.

Peculiarities of Marketing Cost of Forest Produce

- Forest produce is scattered over wide area assembling of small lots into sizable work is an additional job.
- Forest product is vary much in quality and hence they need to be graded as to confirm to certain well-established standards.
- Forest products are bulky and perishable in nature and hence, become more difficult to transport and to store.
- Longer period of waiting (long gestation period) involve in case of forest product before the money invested in forestry could be realized.
- Margin of the marketing agencies appears to be more.

Objectives of Studying Marketing Cost

- To ascertain as to what intermediate agencies intervene between producer and final consumer of the commodity, services they render and margin, they get for such services and to examine whether such services are necessary.
- To ascertain total cost of marketing of a commodity.
- To see whether there is an alternative in order to lower the cost of marketing.
- To compare the price paid by consumer with that price received by grower.

Meaning of Market Margin

Market Margin refers to the difference between price paid and price received by any specific marketing agency, such as single retailer or wholesale retailer or combination of marketing agencies.

Meaning of Price Spread

Distribution of the market price paid by the ultimate consumer (consumer price) among the producer and various intermediaries involved in marketing is known as **price spread.** Distribution of price spread gives us an idea about relative efficiency about various products.

Formulae:

Producer shares in consumer rupee (% share) $= \dfrac{\text{Net Price received by grower}}{\text{Amount paid by consumer}} \times 100$

Price spread $= \dfrac{\text{Price received by producer}}{\text{price paid by consumer}} \times 100$

Total Marketing Cost = Amount paid by consumer- net price received by grower

Gross added value = sale value of process material- price of raw material

Net added value = gross added value – processing charges

% gross added value = Gross added value/original value * 100

% Net added value = net added value/original value * 100

Example : A forest produce *Bixa orellana* seed reached from producer to ultimate consumer through different middlemen. The whole quantity of the same is sold and purchased at various prices by different agencies. Based on the following information, calculate total marketing cost, price spread, net received to producer, producer share in consumer rupee, margin of wholeseller and also show its route:

1. Gross price received by producer is Rs. 2200.00, 2. Expenses incurred by producer for transportation and handling charges is Rs. 262, 3. Price paid by retailer to whole seller is Rs. 2500.00, 4. Expenses incurred by wholeseller is Rs. 125.00, 5. Price paid by consumer is Rs. 2750.00

Price Spread

The difference between the price paid by the consumer and the price received by the producer for an equivalent commodity is known as **price spread**; sometimes this is termed as **marketing margin**.

Three methods are used in the estimation of price spread

1. Lot Method

A specific lot or consignment is selected and chased through the marketing system until it reaches the ultimate consumer. The cost and margin involved at each stage are assessed and added to get the price spread.

Limitations of Lot Method

1. It is difficult to chase the movement of a lot from the producer to the ultimate consumer.
2. Most of the lots lose their identity because either the product gets processed or lot gets mixed up with other lots.
3. There is no assurance that the lot selected is representative of the whole product. This method is appropriate for perishable commodities like vegetables, fruits and milk.

2. Sum of Average Gross Margin Method

The average gross margins of all the intermediaries are added to obtain the total marketing margin as well as the breakup of the consumer's rupee. The following formula may be used to work out the total marketing margins :

$$M_T = \sum_{i=1}^{n} \left[\frac{Si - Pi}{Qi} \right]$$

where, MT = Total marketing margin Si = Sale value of a product for i^{th} intermediary Pi = Purchase value paid by the ith intermediary Qi = Quantity of the product handled by the ith intermediary i = 1, 2 ..N {number of intermediaries involved in the marketing channel

Difficulties in using this method are :

1. Traders may not allow access to their account books because they may make false entries to evade sales and income tax.
2. This method necessitates adjustment for the difference between the quantities purchased and sold because a part of the product is wasted during handling.

3. Comparison of Prices at Successive Levels of Marketing

Under this method prices at successive stages of marketing at the producer, wholesaler and retailer level are compared. The margin of an intermediary is worked out by deducting the ascertainable costs incurred by that intermediary.

The difficulties in the use of the this method are :

1. Representative and comparable series of prices for the same quality at successive stages of marketing are not readily available for all the products.
2. Adjustment for loss in the quality of the product at various stages of marketing due to wastage and spoilage in processing and handling is difficult.
3. The time lag between the performances of various marketing operations is not properly accounted.

❑❑❑

Chapter 5

Concepts of Market Integration and Marketing Efficiency

Market Integration

Meaning

Integration is an attempt at organizing or coordinating the marketing processes to increase operational efficiency and acquire greater power over the selling and/or buying process.

Integration shows the relationship of firms in a market. The extent of integration influences the market conduct of the firms and consequently their marketing efficiency. Markets differ in the extent of integration and, therefore, there is a variation in their degree of efficiency.

Market integration is a process which refers to the expansion of firms by consolidating additional marketing functions and activities under a single management.

Khols and Uhl's have defined marketing integration as process which refers to the expansion of firm by consolidating additional marketing function and activity under single management.

For example,

i) Establishment of wholesaling facilities by NTFP retailers.

ii) Setting up of another extraction unit by the biofuel processor.

Types of Market Integration: There are three basic kinds of market integration :

1. Horizontal Integration
2. Vertical Integration
3. Conglomeration

1. Horizontal Integration

In this type of integration, some marketing agencies (say sellers) combine to form a union to reduce their effective number and the extent of actual competition in the market. e.g. Primary milk producers co-operative society.

This occurs when a firm or agencies gains control of others firms or agencies performing similar marketing functions at the same level in the marketing sequence. In this some marketing agencies combine to form a union with a view to reducing their effective number and the extent of actual competition in the market. In this arrangement, there are four firms engaged in buying and selling of timber under the direction of the parent forest based business firm. All the four business firms perform the same type of marketing function but their location and area of operation are different. The schematic arrangement of Horizontally Integrated Firms can be as follows :

The horizontal integration of firms may be actuated by the following motives:

i) Buying out a competitor in a time bound way to reduce competition
ii) Gaining a larger share of the market and higher profits
iii) Attaining economics of scale
iv) Specializing in the trade
v) Horizontal integration in the food industry is limited because of its potential impact on competition.

2. Vertical Integration

Vertical integration occurs, when a firm performs more than one activity in the sequence of the marketing process. It is linking together of two or more functions in the marketing process within a single firm or under a single ownership.

For e.g. If a firm assumes wholesale as well as retailing, it is a vertical integration or rice processor undertaking retailing.

It occurs when a firm performs more than one activity in the sequence of marketing process. A combination of agencies or activities is related to each other and linking together two or more functions in the marketing process within a single firm or under a single ownership.

e.g. Timber harvesting contractor also engage in purchasing of timber, saw milling, transportation, selling, etc.

Parent Forest Business Firm'→ A. Wholesaling **B.**Transportation **C.**Harvesting **D.**Saw milling

The schematic arrangement of Vertically Integrated Firms can be as follows :

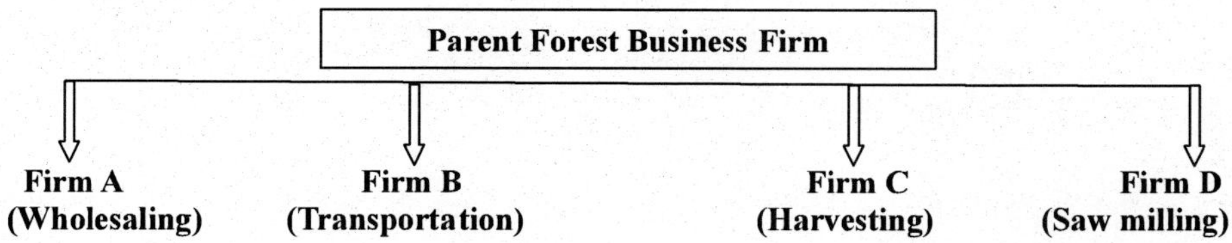

The vertical integration of firms may be actuated by the following motives:

i) More profits by taking up additional functions

ii) Risk education through improved market coordination

iii) Improvement in bargaining power and the prospects of influencing prices

iv) Lowering costs through achieving operational efficiency

3. Conglomeration

A combination of agencies or activities which are not directly related to each other may operate under a unified management be termed as **conglomeration.**

Examples of conglomeration are ITC, Birla Group, J. K. Group, Delhi Cloth and General Mills (cloth and vanaspathi), NAFED-National Agricultural Co-operative Marketing Federation of India.

The schematic arrangement of Conglomeration can be as follows:

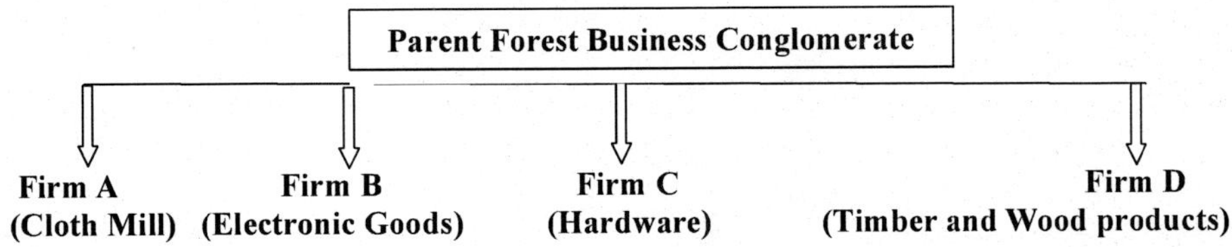

The conglomerate is involved in a number of different and frequently unrelated activities. e.g. A firm dealing with forestry products, processing of horticultural products, cloth milling, selling and repairs of electronic equipments, manufacturer of vanaspati and a chain of retail outlets. Such a conglomeration of activities serves as a means of spreading the risk and helps in expanding the activities to additional markets.

The conglomeration integration of firms may be actuated by the following motives:

i) Risk reduction through diversification

ii) Acquisition of financial leverage

iii) Empire building urge

Degree of Integration

There are two types of integration based on degree of integration:

1. Ownership Integration

This occurs, when all the decision and assets of a firm are completely assumed by another firm. e.g. Ownership integration is a processing firm which buys a wholesaling firm or a retailer chain.

2. Contract Integration

This involves agreements between two firms on certain decisions, while each firm retains its separate identity.

e.g. Tie up of a saw mill with timber trade for supply of timber.

Contract farming is a typical case of integration between farmers and processors or retailers (chains)

Marketing efficiency

Meaning of Marketing Efficiency

The term 'marketing efficiency' refers to the effectiveness or competence with which a market structure performs its designated function.

Khol's and Uhl's defined Marketing Efficiency as the ratio of market output (satisfaction) to marketing inputs (cost of resources). An increase in this ratio represents improved efficiency and a decrease denotes reduced efficiency.

$$\left[E = \frac{O}{I} \times 100\right]$$

Jasadanwala defined it as the effectiveness or competence with which a market structure performs its designation function.

Efficient marketing

A reduction in marketing cost without reduction in consumer satisfaction indicates improvement in efficiency. A higher level of consumer satisfaction at higher marketing cost may mean increased efficiency, if the additional satisfaction derived by consumer outweighs the additional cost incurred on the marketing process. But a change that reduces cost but also reduces consumer satisfaction need not indicate increase in marketing efficiency.

The efficient marketing system for forest product ensure that :

1. Increase in the farm production is translated into a proportionate increase in the level of real income in the economy, thereby stimulating the emergence of additional surplus.
2. Good production years do not coincide with low revenues to the producers achieved through effective storage, proper regional distribution and channellizing of latent (hidden) demand.
3. Consumer derives the greatest possible satisfaction at the least possible cost.

Approaches to the assessment of marketing efficiency

Efficiency of marketing system could be looked at two angles :

1. Technical or physical or operational efficiency
2. Pricing or allocative efficiency.

1. Technical Efficiency

Efficiency is said to have increased, when cost is reduced for performing a function for each unit of output. This can be brought out by reducing physical losses or through change in technology of the function *viz.* storage, transportation, handling and processing. A change in the technique may result in the reduction of per unit cost (e.g. storage cost for a month, transportation cost to a distance of 100 kms or the cost of converting 100 kg of Garcinia fruits to kokum juice) or the increase in the output for a given level of cost.

2. Pricing Efficiency

Pricing efficiency means that the system is able to allocate farm products either over time, across the space or among the traders; processors and consumers in such a way that no other allocation would make producers and consumers better off. This is achieved *via* pricing of the product at different stages at different places, at different time and among different users and hence, called pricing efficiency. In simple terms, the pricing efficiency is achieved, when following conditions hold:

a) Price differences between spatially separated markets do not exceed transportation cost.

b) Intra-year price rise is not more than storage cost.

c) Price differences between forms of the product do not exceed processing cost. e.g. Amla fruits and amla pickles, Teak logs and teak furnitures, wheat grain and wheat flour.

The above two types of efficiencies are mutually reinforcing in the long run, one without the other is not enough.

For examples :

i) Farmers expect quick market clearance and higher prices for their produce. They expect the market to buy the products, when they are offered for sale at reasonable prices.

ii) Consumers expect ready availability of products in the form and quality desired by them at lower prices.

iii) Traders and other functionaries expect steady and increasing incomes.

iv) Government expect the system to safeguard the interest of all the three sections and in a proportion which is considered to be fair so that overall long run welfare of the society is maximized.

Empirical Assessment of Marketing Efficiency

Some simple measures to assess the efficiency of the marketing system for a forestry/agricultural/horticultural commodities are:

1. Ratio of Output to Input

Efficiency of any activity or process is defined as the ratio of output to input. If "O" and "I" are respectively output and input of the marketing system and "E" is the index of marketing efficiency, then E = (O/I) x 100. A higher value of E denotes higher level of efficiency and vice versa.

Consider the following examples of marketing efficiency :

Let there be two markets (or channels), A and B, for any NTFP commodity. This NTFP produce moves in both the markets. Let the marketing costs and value added in above markets be as given below. The efficiency measure is calculated as illustrated in below table.

The below table depicts that market B is more efficient than market A, though marketing cost is higher in market B. But this conclusion is may be misleading. It can be argued that consumers were charged three times the actual cost of marketing in market B, whereas they were charged only twice in market A. Market B infact could be less efficient than market A. One needs to go into the question of degree of competition in two markets.

Marketing Efficiency of Two Hypothetical Markets (A and B)

Sl. No.	Particulars	Market A	Market B
1.	Total marketing cost incurred by all those involved (Rs./ton)	300	500
2.	Value added measured in terms of difference in the consumer's price and price received by the farmer (Rs./ton)	600	1500
3.	Marketing efficiency	200	300

2. Shepherd Approach

Shepherd suggested that the **"ratio of the total value of goods marketed to the marketing cost"** may be used as a measure of marketing efficiency. Higher the ratio, the higher efficiency and vice versa. This method eliminates the problem of measurement of value added. Consider the following example of working out the marketing efficiency of banana market using the Shepherd's formula:

The banana in Andhra Pradesh is sold either to the pre-harvest contractors or directly in the market eliminating the pre-harvest contractors. The costs and margins on sale of banana are shown in the below table.

Table: Estimates of marketing costs, margins and marketing efficiency for banana in Guntur District of Andhra Pradesh.

Particulars	Channel I (Contract sale)	Channel II (Direct sale)
1. Marketing costs incurred by producers	-	436.02
2. Marketing costs incurred by pre-harvest contractor	428.61	-
3. Margin of pre-harvest contractor	253.28	-
4. Marketing costs incurred by retailer	160.09	160.09
5. Marketing margin of retailer	308.25	308.25
6. Total costs and margins	1150.23	904.36
7. Retailer's sale price or consumer's purchase price	2106.38	2106.38
8. Net price received by the producer (7-6)	956.15	1202.02
9. Shepherd's index of marketing efficiency (7÷6)	1.83	2.32
10. 7 ÷ (1+2+4)	3.58	3.53

The table shows that the marketing efficiency of Channel II is more than that of Channel I.

3. Acharya Approach

This measure of marketing efficiency is used for comparing the efficiency of alternate markets/channels, which takes into account all the following:

a) Total marketing costs (MC)
b) Net marketing margin (MM)
c) Prices received by the farmer (FP)
d) Prices paid by the consumer (RP)

Further, the measure should reflect the following relationship between each of these variables and the marketing efficiency :

i) Higher the MC, lower the efficiency
ii) Higher the MM, lower the efficiency
iii) Higher the FP, higher the efficiency
iv) Higher the RP, lower the efficiency

As there is an exact relationship among four variables, i.e. a+b+c=d, any three of these could be used to arrive at a measure for comparing the marketing efficiency. The following modified measure is suggested by Acharya:

Modified Marketing Efficiency = MME = FP ÷ (MC+MM)

Where, FP- Prices received by the farmer, **MC-** Total marketing costs (MC), MM - Net marketing margin

Table: Measurement of marketing efficiency: Alternative Approaches

Sl. No.	Particulars	Unit	Market A (Channel A)	Market B (Channel B)	Market C (Channel C)
1.	Retailer's sale price or consumer's purchase price (RP)	Rs/q	1000	1000	1000
2.	Total marketing costs (MC)	Rs/q	300	500	300
3.	Total net margins of intermediaries (MM)	Rs/q	200	100	400
4.	Net price received by the farmers (FP)	Rs/q	500	400	300
5.	Value added (S.No. 1–4)	Rs/q	500	600	700
Index of marketing efficiency					
a)	Conventional method [E= 5 ÷2]	Rs/q	1.67	1.20	2.33
b)	Shepherd's method [ME = 1÷2]	Rs/q	3.33	2.00	3.33
c)	Acharya's method [MME = 4÷(2+3)]	Rs/q	1.00	0.67	0.43

A comparison of efficiency measures as worked out by three different methods is given in the table below. The conventional method (E) suggests that market C is more efficient than market A which, in turn, is more efficient than market B. Note that the price received by the farmer in market C is the lowest. Hence, this method is not suitable under Indian conditions.

If marketing margins are not included as a part of marketing cost, the Shepherd method (ME) suggests that market A and market C are equally efficient. Further, these two markets are more efficient than market B. The limitation of this method is that it does not take into account of the price received by the farmer.

The limitations of both of these methods are taken care by the modified method, suggested by Acharya. According to Acharya's method (MME), market A is more efficient than market B which, in turn, is more efficient than market C. Acharya's measure of marketing efficiency can also be stated as $MME = [RP \div (MC + MM)]^{-1}$

$RP = FP + MC + MM$

❑❑❑

Chapter 6

Role of Government and Private Agencies in Marketing of Forest Produce

Agencies/Institutions involved in Marketing of the Forest Produce

1. **NOVOD -** National Oilseeds and Vegetable oils Development Board, Gurgaon, Haryana.
2. **ISI** - Indian Standard Institution (1947). It is re-named as Bureau of Indian Standard (BIS), New Delhi (1987)
3. **NHB -** National Horticulture Board (1984), Gurgaon.
4. **Spice Board -** Cochin (1987)
5. **COSAMB -** Council of State Agriculture Marketing Board (1988)
6. **NCDC -** National Co-operative Development Corporation, New Delhi, (1976)
7. **FCI -** Food Corporation of India, New Delhi (1964)
8. **TDC -** Tribal Development Corporation, New Delhi (1972)
9. **FDCM -** Forest Development Corporation of Maharashtra Limited, Nagpur (1974)
10. **TMFI -** Tribals Mission Foundation International, Philippines (1985)
11. **TRIFED -** Tribal Co-operative Marketing Development Federation of India Limited, New Delhi (1987),
12. **STDC -** State Tribal Development Corporation, Mumbai (1972)
13. **MFPTDFS -** Minor Forest Product (Trading and Development) Federations (1992)
14. **STDCCS -** State Tribal Development Co-operative Corporations (1992)

15. **NIAM** – National Institute of Agricultural Marketing, Jaipur (1988)
16. **NAFED** - National Agricultural Co-operative Marketing Federation of India
17. **NMPB** – National Medicinal Plant Board, New Delhi (2000)
18. **APEDA** – Agricultural Processed Products and Export Development Agency, New Delhi (1986)
19. **TRTI** – Tribal Research and Training Institute, Pune (1962)
20. **MSCTDC** - Maharashtra State Co-operative Tribal Development Corporation, Nashik (1972)
21. **MSAMB** - Maharashtra State Agricultural Marketing Board, Pune (1984)
22. **AGMARK** - Agricultural Marketing, Nagpur (1953) (Symbol of Agril. Marketing on graded products).
23. **NABARD** – National Bank for Agriculture and Rural Development.
24. **KIAM** – Karnataka Institute of Agricultural Marketing, Mysore.
25. **NDDB** – National Dairy Development Board, Anand, Gujarat.
26. **TANFED** – Tamil Nadu Co-operative Marketing Federation Ltd (Popularly known as TANFED)
27. **MPEDA** - Marine Products Exports Development Authority.

Forest Development Corporations

After the recommendation in the Interim Report of the National Commission on Agriculture **(NCA, 1972)** on **'Production of Man-made Forests'**, many State Governments in India established **Forest Development Corporations (FDCs)** to work on commercial lines by raising industrial plantations of teak, eucalyptus, bamboo, etc., to enhance the production of forest produce, to restore the productivity of degraded forest areas, to harvest and undertake trade to timber and Non-Timber Forest Products (NTFPs), to own and run forest based industries, to provide support to farmers for marketing their forest product, and to provide consultancy in raising bio-aesthetic plantations, etc. Most of the FDC were created during 1970s.

FDCs exists in 22 states (except in Assam, Manipur, Mizoram, Nagaland, Rajasthan and Sikkim) and in the UT of Andaman & Nicobar Island. Most of the states have only one FDC but two states have more than one forest related corporation, namely Karnataka (Karnantaka FDC, Forest Industries Corporation, & Cashew Development Corporation).

1. **Andhra Pradesh: Andhra Pradesh Forest Development Corporation (APFDC)** established in 1975 has an annual turnover of about Rs. 60 crore at present.
2. **Andaman & Nicobar Island: Forest Plantation and Development Corporation**, a Government of India undertaking, was established in 1977, mainly to harvest timber, to manage the inaccessible forest and to undertake cultivation of red oil palm, rubber, spices, etc.
3. **Arunachal Pradesh: Arunachal Pradesh Forest Corporation** was established in 1977, mainly to harvest and market timber in the leased forest area by the Forest Department in Tirap and Changlang districts of the state as well as to establish a few wood based industries.
4. **Bihar: Bihar Forest Development Corporation (FDC)** was established in 1975, mainly for harvesting and marketing of NTEPs of which tendu leaf was a major product.
5. **Chhattisgarh**: Though **FDC was created in 1976, after bifurcation of the state from Madhya Pradesh in 2000,** it was re-established in 2001, and the annual turnover is of about Rs. 45 crore at present.
6. **Gujarat: The FDC was created in 1976** has an annual turnover of about Rs. 30 crore.
7. **Haryana: Haryana Forest Development Corporation (HFDC)** was established in December 1989 under the Companies Act, 1956. The annual turnover is of the order of Rs. 37 crore at present.
8. **Himachal Pradesh: Himahcal Pradesh State Forest Development Corporation** was established in 1974. The turnover at present is about Rs. 150 crore with approximate profit of Rs. 15 crore.

9. **Jammu and Kashmir**: **The Jammu & Kashmir State Forest Corporation**, a statutory body, was established under the Jammu and Kashmir State Forest Corporation Act, 1978.

10. **Jharkhand**: **Jharkhand Forest Development Corporation** was re-established in 2002 after bifurcation of the state from Bihar to carry on the earlier activities of the Bihar Forest Corporation mainly to harvest NTEPs.

11. **Karnataka**:

    i) **The Karnataka Forest Development Corporation (KFDC)** was established in 1971 with the main objective to raise plantations to commercially viable species (rubber, pulpwood, teak and bamboo).

    ii) **The Karnataka State Forest Industries Corporation** was incorporated in the year 1973, under the Companies Act, 1956 with the main objective to harvest forest produce for supply to pulpwood and rayon industries, processing of wood, and manufacture of furniture and wood based construction material.

    iii) **Karnataka Cashew Development Corporation** was incorporated in 1978, under the Companies' Act, 1956, with the main objective of taking over the existing cashew plantation for intensive development and to raise new cashew plantation in the state to attain increased productivity.

12. **Kerala**: **Kerala Forest Development Corporation** was established in 1975, in Kottayam with specific purpose to raise industrial plantations, spices, cashew, tea, coffee, etc. and to process and trade.

13. **Madhya Pradesh**: **Madhya Pradesh Rajya Van Vikas Nigam** was established in 1975 with the main objective to replace low value and inferior forests with high value multi utility species.

14. **Maharashtra**: The FDC created in 1974 has an annual turnover of about Rs. 130 crore at present.

15. **Meghalaya**: Meghalaya FDC was established in 1975 under Companies Act, 1956 with authorized share capital of Rs. 2 crore mainly to harvest timber from government forests and to enter into timber trade.

16. **Odisha**: Odisha FDC came into being in 1990 by merging all forest corporations of the state which include Odisha Forest Corporation (1962).
17. **Punjab: The Punjab State Forest Development Corporation** was established in 1983 under the Companies Act, 1956, and the annual turnover is nearly Rs. 34 crore, at present.
18. **Tamil Nadu**:
    i) **Tamil Nadu Forest Plantation Corporation Limited (TAFCORN)** was incorporated under the provisions of the Companies Act, 1956 and 1974 with the main objective to raise, maintain and harvest pulpwood and cashew to meet the needs of industries and to supply firewood to meet the fuelwood needs of the public.
    ii) **Arasu Rubber Corporation** is a Government of Tamil Nadu Company functioning under the Tamil Nadu Company functioning under the Tamil Nadu Department of Environment and Forest since 20th August, 1984.
    iii) **Tamil Nadu Tea Plantation Corporation Limited (TANTEA)**, an undertaking of the State Government of Tamil Nadu, India was established in 1968, to re-habilitate Sri Lankan repatriates trained in the fine art of tea culture.
19. **Tripura: Tripura Forest Development and Plantation Corporation Limited (TFDPC)** was established in the year 1976 under the Companies Act, 1956, and the present turnover is Rs. 45 crore with net profit of Rs. 16 crore.
20. **Uttar Pradesh: Uttar Pradesh Forest Corporati**on was established in 1974 under State's Local Bodies Act and not under Company's Act like other States FDCs. The annual turnover is of the order of Rs. 300 crore at present.
21. **Uttarakhand**: Till the creation as a separate state in November 2000, the activities of Uttar Pradesh Forest Corporation were extended in Uttarakhand. After the creation of a separate state, **Uttarakhand Forest Corporation** was established in 2001, and the activities identical to UP Forest Corporation have been continuing.
22. **West Bengal: The West Bengal Forest Development Corporation (WBFDC)** came into existence in 1974 and has an annual turnover of Rs. 90 crore & net profit of about Rs. 5 crore.

Role of Government Agencies in Marketing of Forest Produce

1. Framing rules and regulations for the protection of the interest of some section of the population, which relate to restrict the activities of traders, licensees and market regulation.
2. Creation of marketing infrastructure, such as storage (warehousing), transportation and communication facilities.
3. Administration of price at different level of marketing. Generating minimum support price (MSP) to producer, providing commodities at fair prices to consumer and fixing the rate of commission charged by commission agent.
4. Balancing supply and demand by regulating import, internal procurement and distribution.
5. Establishment of organization to provide services to the farmers for performing certain marketing functions.
6. Promotions of farmer's co-operation societies for forest marketing and forest processing.
7. Market survey and research.
8. Market Extension.
9. Promotion of grading and standardization.
10. Market intelligence.
11. Training to market personnel.
12. To prevent the exploitation of farmers.
13. To make marketing system most effective and efficient, so that farmers may get better price for their produce and goods, which are made available to consumer at seasonal prices.
14. To provide intensive prices to farmers to increase the production.
15. Carrying out marketing cost and market margin studies by mapping out the channels for produces of their respective areas.
16. Identifying the variety of crops and their areas.
17. To check herding, black marketing and profiting.
18. To maintain sizable buffer stock of food grains.
19. To make timely release of stock through public distribution system.
20. To help in import and export of goods.

Tribal Co-operative Marketing Development Federation of India Ltd (TRIFED), New Delhi (Ministry of Tribal Affairs, Govt. of India)

Introduction

The Tribal Cooperative Marketing Development Federation of India (TRIFED) came into existence in 1987. It is a national-level apex organization functioning under the administrative control of Ministry of Tribal Affairs, Govt. of India. TRIFED has its registered and Head Office located in New Delhi and has a network of 13 Regional Offices located at various places in the country.

Government of India set up ***TRIFED in 1987***. TRIFED is an apex-level federation of State Tribal Development Co-operative Federation and State Corporations. A head quarter is at New Delhi. It has its own wide network agencies throughout the country for the procurement, processing and marketing of forest and agricultural commodities produced in the tribal areas of the country. TRIFED has branch offices spread across various states of India, the major one being in Mumbai, Chennai, Calcutta, Hyderabad, Udaipur, Guwahati, Ranchi, Bhopal and Bhubaneswar. While procuring commodities from the tribals, TRIFED has to overcome the problems of poor communication, lack of access, poor economies of scale and perishability of goods. Its procurement operations cover the whole country either directly or through its associates at the doorstep of tribal people. TRIFED's procurement policy framework also provides price support for tribal people and protects them against exploitative market forces by influencing the latter to pay prices at par with the prices paid by TRIFED.

TRIFED has aggressively undertaken procurement and marketing of over 80 items of tribal produce, which are environment - friendly, fresh, pure and 100% natural to secure higher earnings and generate employment opportunities for tribal people.

Objectives of TRIFED

- To improve tribals standard of living
- To pay specific attention to the marketing requirements of tribal forest and agriculture produce.

- To conserve nation's ecological heritage, of which the tribals are guardians, which needs to be given due importance.
- To ensure assured off-take of their products and remunerative prices while eliminating exploitation of tribals by market forces.
- To create awareness of interplay of market forces among tribals to enable them to optimize their incomes
- To provide assured markets and remunerative prices for tribal produce and also undertake price support operations, wherever required.
- To upgrade the quality of tribal products with a view to maximize unit value realization
- To export tribal products
- To provide full range of services, including organization and collection of tribal produce, scientific exploration of forest products, storage, transportation, marketing and exports.

Tribes India Outlets

TRIFED is engaged in procurement and marketing of tribal art and craft items through its chain of 40 retail outlets called "**TRIBES INDIA**", which offers a range of tribal products, which include:

Metal Craft	**Tribal Textiles**	**Jewellery**	**Tribal Paintings**
Cane & Bamboo	**Pottery**	**Gifts and Novelties**	**Organic and Natural Products**

Through this initiative TRIFED provides a platform through which tribals products can be marketed in retail directly to the consumers and in the process ensures that tribal gets a fair price.

TRIFED has won the National Award for excellence in training for the year 2015 for improving efficiency and effectiveness of the skill development and capacity building of MFPs gatherers training programmes. The total outlay for the scheme is Rs 967 crore as centre's share for the plan period during 2013-14 to 2016-17.

Minimum Support Price Scheme (MSPS)

MFP contributes to livelihoods and alleviating poverty of nearly 100 million people. Ensuring fair returns to these poor people is duty of the State. The people who depend on MFP are also beset with a number of other problems, such as perishable nature of the produce, lack of holding capacity, lack of marketing infrastructure, exploitation by middlemen, lack of Government intervention at the required time and scale, volatile nature of markets, etc. Consequently, the MFP gatherers who are mostly poor are unable to bargain for fair prices. Government. of India has taken a number of initiatives for socio-economic development of tribals and recognizing the critical importance which MFP hold for tribals and its potential to create large scale employment opportunities thereby helping in reducing poverty and increasing empowerment of tribals particularly women and poor people in backward districts of the country, Govt. of India has decided to introduce the scheme of "Mechanism for Marketing of Minor Forest Produce (MFP) through Minimum Support Price (MSP) and development of value chain". The scheme is designed as a social safety net for improvement of livelihood of MFP gatherers by providing them fair price for the MFPs they collect.

The scheme has been started with following objectives:

- To provide fair price to the MFP gatherers for the produce collected by them and enhance their income level
- To ensure sustainable harvesting of MFPs.

The Scheme will have a huge social dividend for MFP gatherers, majority of whom are tribals. It is a holistic scheme for development of MFP trade including its value chain and necessary infrastructure at local level. The MSP scheme seeks to establish a framework to ensure fair returns for the produce collected by tribals, assurance of buying at a particular price, primary processing, storage, transportation, etc. while ensuring sustainability of the resource base.

Private Marketing Agencies

Merchant middlemen: They are those individuals who take title of the goods they handle. They buy and sell on their own and gain or lose depending on the difference in the sale and purchase prices. Merchant middlemen are of two types-wholesaler and retailers.

Wholesalers: They buy and sell food grains in large quantities. They may buy directly from farmers or from other wholesalers. They sell food grains either in the same market or in other markets. They sell to retailers, other wholesalers and processors. They do not sell significant quantities to ultimate consumers. They own godown for the storage of the produce.

Retailers buy goods from wholesalers and sell them to consumers in small quantity. They are producers, personal representatives to consumers. Retailers are closest to consumers in the marketing channel.

Itinerant traders are petty merchants who move from village to village and directly purchase the produce from the cultivators. They transport it to the nearby primary or secondary market and sell it there.

Village merchants have their small establishments in villages. They purchase the produce of those farmers who have either taken finance from them or those who are not able to go to the market. They often visit nearby markets and keep in touch with the prevailing prices. They either sell the collected produce in nearby market or retain it for sale at a later date in the village itself.

Agent Middle men act as representative of their clients. They do not take title of the produce, and therefore, do not own it. They merely negotiate the purchase and/ or sale. They sell services to their principals and not the goods or commodities. They receive income in the form of commission or brokerage. They sere as buyers or sellers in the effective bargaining. Agent middlemen are of two types, commission agents and brokers.

A **Commission Agent** normally takes over the physical handling of the produce, arranges for its sale, collects the prices, from the buyer, deducts his expenses to the seller. All these facilities are extended to buyer firm as well, if asked for.

Brokers render personal services to their clients in the market but unlike the commission agents, they do not have physical control of the product. The main function of a broker is to bring together buyer and sellers on the same platform for negotiations. Their charge is called brokerage.

They may claim brokerage from the buyer and seller or both, depending upon the market situation and the service rendered. They have no establishments in the market. They have complete knowledge of the market of quantity available and prevailing prices.

Speculative Middlemen take title to the product with a view to make a profit on it. They are not regular buyer or sellers of produce. They specialize in risk taking. They buy at lower prices when arrivals are substantial and sell in the off-season, when prices are high. They do the minimum handling of the goods. They make a profit from the short run as well as long run price fluctuations.

Processors carry on their business either on their own or on custom basis. Some processors employ agents to buy for them in the producing areas, store the produce and process it throughout the year on continuous basis. They also engage in advertising activity to create a demand for the processed products.

Facilitative Middlemen, some middlemen do not buy and sell directly but assist in the marketing process. Marketing can take place even if they are not active. But the efficiency of marketing systems increases when they are engaged in business, these middlemen receive their income in the form of fees from those who use their services. The important facilitative middlemen are labourers, weigh men, graders, transport agency, communication agency and advertising agency.

Market inefficiencies in the trade of forest produce and measures to check the same

Problems of marketing and measures to overcome

Introduction

Various non-wood forest produce belongs to forest department and are collected from the forest area. In India, few rights are given to tribals for collection and use of forest product. In some states like Kerala, tribals are allowed to collect medicinal plants at concessional rate. The exploitive middleman can be overcome by establishment of **forest labour co-operative society** and **tribal labour co-operative society**. The NWFP collected by these societies may be purchased by forest corporation department, which processes to market and prepare finished goods and products. In this way tribal receives more economic returns. The society collects the medicinal plants and market through the forest based industries, co-operation and also market federations.

In the tribal areas of our country, NWFP are collected by the tribal development corporation (TDC). The state government has given the concession to TDC to collect and transport the specified NWFP without payment or royalty. The TDC and other co-operation dealing with the NWFP have processing unit to add value to the collected production. The NWFP in market surplus are mostly sold as standing crop.

Problems of Forest Marketing

1. Most NWFPs are sold without processing and value addition. The producer's access to consumer is limited to sell to local village and weekly market. A major portion of their product is sold to intermediate like contractor or agent who operates in the area.
2. The limitation in access to market is more pronounced in case of handicraft and products from cottage industry. The market is geographically distributed over wide area and remains inaccessible.
3. Small size of their production and collection.
4. Limited access to market and the dependence on intermediatories have a direct effect on price.
5. Sustainable supply of produce to manufacturing company.
6. Services provided by middleman.
7. Lack of information on current market channel, amount of each product, price variation, supply and demand.
8. Proper communication facilities.
9. Proper market place for selling forest produce.
10. Middle man and contractor often take advantage of collectors' ignorance of actual market rate and collector inability to hold or store their collection for longer period.
11. Packaging of forest produce.
12. Transportation facilities
13. Storage facilities
14. Processing facilities
15. Marketable and market surplus
16. Marketing efficiency
17. Marketing cost, margin and price spread
18. Market regulation.

Measures to Overcome Forest Marketing Problems

- Local management of forest through Joint Forest Management (JFM).
- Co-operation or community organization provide good marketing information

- Involvement of government agencies
- Removal of regulation on collection, price, transport and handling of NTFP.
- **Competition -** The more buyers are better, if price information is available for the produce/collector, competition between middlemen will result in a better price and better survival.
- **Marketed analysis** - The flow of each product from collection to consumer must be studied, so that the information needed for sustainable management, fair price and efficient market can be made available.
- Suitable structure of support prices for various farm commodities should be adjusted from time to time.
- Adequate arrangement of NTFPs/agricultural produce on support price, if the price falls below the level.
- Regulated infrastructure of markets and warehouses, which ensure fair prices.
- Rural roads must be complimented and coordinated with railways, nearest waterways (port), airports, if possible.
- The efficient marketing is predominantly influenced by efficient distribution system (it means products should reach consumer in the quickest time possible at minimum cost.
- The development of communication systems appropriate to rural market may cost upto six times as much as reaching an urban market through established media, need rural communication facilities.
- The state marketing board or federation or market committees also the producers, traders and sellers have necessarily to be consulted, as they have the principal interest towards its use.
- The arrivals of various products, such as Ffod grains, vegetables, dairy products, flowers, etc. need speedy transport.
- Public weighing machines in each rural market to ensure correct weight both for farm and non-farm arrivals.
- Storage godowns and an official so required. For storage facilities the government should not depend on private agencies to store food grains (National commission on Agriculture recommended).

- Rural markets need more number of godowns and ancillary (low level) platforms for packaging places, market office cum information cell, bank and post office.
- Rural marketing is the nerve center of a rural economy; rural markets are the channels for the movements of goods and services as well as to promote cultural integration.
- Improve physical communication facility throughout the country.
- Rural communication must be in regional language and dialects (sub-language).
- The existing marketing staff must be increased and adequate training must be given.
- Extending of financial support for modernization of the forest-processing units is also needed.
- The proper packaging technology must be improved.

Marketing of Non-Timber Forest Products

Non-timber forest products (NTFP) include game animals, fur-bearers (short fine hair of some animals), nuts and seeds, berries, mushrooms, oils, foliage, medicinal plants, peat (carbonized vegetable matter used for fuel), fuelwood, forage, etc. The policy environment relating to NTFPs in India is characterized by the underlying belief that forests are state property and thus, all products growing in forests are owned by the state. The state's control even extends to designated forest products growing on private lands and non-forest common lands. Thus, bamboo or tendu leaves or mahua flowers on private lands are subjected to the same control, as if growing on forest lands. (hill broom- yellow flowered shrub).

Importance

About 100 million people living in and around forests in India derive their livelihood support from the collection and marketing of non-timber forest products (NTFPs). These NTFPs provide subsistence and farm inputs, such as fuel, food, medicines, fruits, manure, and fodder. The collection of NTFPs is a source of cash income, especially during the slack seasons, because of their increasing commercial importance.

Today, in India, NTFPs provide approximately 40% of total official forest revenues, 55% of forest-based employment, and 70% of the total exports from forest products (Tewari and Campbell, 1997). Also, many NTFPs, such as mahua flowers, hill brooms and tamarind, are consumed or traded locally by the forest dwellers (inhabitants) without contributing much to government revenues.

Restrictions

There are various State Forest Acts which put restrictions on storage, transportation, processing as well as marketing of NTFP. There are laws relating to the amount of NTFP that can be stored whether by gatherers or growers. The law also requires the registration of growers of specified forest products whose production is in excess of the specified quantity. Similarly, for transporting NTFPs, transit permits issued by the forest department are still required for most products for their movements within and outside the State.

Recommendations for Effective Marketing

- Rather than be a monopoly buyer of NTFPs, try to regulate price through administrative mechanisms, government should adopt market-friendly policies and facilitate private trade.
- It should encourage local bulking, storage and processing, and bring large buyers in touch with gatherers, so as to reduce the number of layers of intermediaries.
- Enact a Central Act to ban controls on movement within and between States.
- Phase out of all forms of monopoly purchase.
- Invite private agencies to procure grain within the state.
- The Food Corporation of India could also conduct open market operations within a price band.
- Encourage the formation of self-help groups among the forest dwellers so that such groups are able to bargain better with the trade.
- Create smoother land laws and remove restrictions on purchase of land by non–domiciled.

❑❑❑

Chapter 7

Fundamentals of International Trade Domestic and International Trade in Timber and Non-timber Forestry Outputs

Study of Trade

Meaning of Trade

"Trade means exchange of goods within persons."

Trade means the person dealing commodities for profit i.e. Person's commercial or industrial nature of thinking. The exchange of goods between citizens, persons of different countries is called as **international trade**. This kind of trade across national frontier has grown in size with improved means of transport, railway, aeroplane, has been largely responsible for this increase in volume of trade.

Distinction between International Trade and Internal or Inter Regional Trade

1. Immobility of Factors of Production

Labour and capital don't move as freely from one country to another, as they do within the country; between region and between the same political boundaries, people distribute themselves more or less according to their opportunity.

2. Different Currency

Each country has different currency; India has Rupees, USA-Dollar, Japan-Yen and so on. Buying and selling between nations give rise to complications which is absent in internal trade (usually the currencies are differentiated and convertibility is quite often not automatic).

3. Restrictions on Trade

The trade between different countries is not free, very often there are restrictions imposed by custom duty, exchange, restriction, fixed quotas. e.g. Our own country has import heavy duty on import of motor car, bikes and other luxuries.

4. Ignorance

Knowledge of one country cannot be exactly same as the other country. Difference in culture, language and religion stand in the way of free communication between countries. On the other hand, labour and capital within the border of country freely moves about from one place to another. These factors influence the internal trade differently from international trade.

5. Transport and Insurance Cost

The Cost of Transport and Insurance also checks the free international trade. The greater the distance between two, the greater will be these costs. Frequent wars increase them still more.

Advantages of International Trade

- The productive resources of the world are utilized to the best advantage
- The country is able to consume goods which it cannot produce at all or only at an impossible high cost. This provides better economic welfare and a higher standard of living.
- Shortage in case of famine and the scarcity can be made achieved from imports
- Countries which are economically backward but rich in unused resources are able to develop their industries. Fluctuating price can be controlled by balancing the production.
- Existence of international trade promotes peace and develops social sympathy (Socio-economic status).

Disadvantages of International Trade

- The worst effect of foreign trade on backward countries is the destruction of their handicraft cottage industries.
- The Empire builders (capitalists) follow the traders.

- Dependency on foreign goods creates difficulties during war, when one country is disconnected by another by enemy action or natural calamities.
- Countries which export primary commodities and import manufacturer goods in return are said to be under-developed countries.
- Foreign trade may exhaust natural resources completely of a country.
- Imports of harmful drug and luxurious items may ruin (affect) the health of nation.
- Through foreign trade, the economic problems of one country are transmitted to others.
- Trade rivalry leads to war and friction and also leads to introduction of pest, weeds, plant, diseases (e.g. Parthenium weeds)

Timber Trade in India

India has about 16% of the world's population. The geographical area accounts for 2.47% and however, the forest area is only 1.8% of the world's forest. A huge human population, coupled with more than 500 million of livestock, exerts immense pressure on its natural resources, including forests.

India is likely to face severe shortage of supply of timber to meet its requirement from both domestic and international front. It is estimated that the demand for timber is likely to grow from 58 million cubic metres in 2005 to 153 million cubic metres in 2020. The supply of wood is projected to increase from 29 million cubic metres in 2000 to 60 million cubic metres in 2020. **The productivity of timber in India is only 0.7 cu. m/ha/year, whereas the world average is 2.1 cu.m/ha/year.** The supply of timber is mainly from forest plantations and wood production is showing a negative growth rate. In the absence of adequate supply from domestic sources, the nation has to depend heavily on imports to meet its demand for timber. This will increase the nation's forest footprint, particularly in South East Asia. In order to minimize the forest footprint, we need to encourage sustainable consumption of timber by promoting forest certification.

Growing Stock of Indian forest is 74.42 m^3/ha

MAI of Indian forests is 0.7 m^3/ha/yr

MAI of World forests is 2.1 m^3/ha/yr

International Trade

International trade : International trade is the exchange of capital, goods, and services across international borders or territories. In most countries, such trade represents a significant share of gross domestic product (GDP).

Industrialization, advanced in technology transportation, globalization, multinational corporations, and outsourcing are all having a major impact on the international trade system. Increasing international trade is crucial to the continuance of globalization. Without international trade, nations would be limited to the goods and services produced within their own borders.

International trade is, in principle, not different from domestic trade as the motivation and the behaviour of parties involved in a trade do not change fundamentally regardless of whether trade is across a border or not. The main difference is that international trade is typically more costly than domestic trade. The reason is that a border typically imposes additional costs such as tariffs, time costs due to border delays and costs, associated with country differences, such as language, the legal system or culture.

Another difference between domestic and international trade is that factors of production, such as capital and labour are typically more mobile within a country than across countries. Thus, international trade is mostly restricted to trade in goods and services, and only to a lesser extent to trade in capital, labour or other factors of production. Trade in goods and services can serve as a substitute for trade in factors of production.

Instead of importing a factor of production, a country can import goods that make intensive use of that factor of production and thus embody it. An example is the import of labour-intensive goods by the United States from China. Instead of importing Chinese labour, the United States imports goods that were produced with Chinese labour. One report in 2010 suggested that international trade was increased when a country hosted a network of immigrants, but the trade effect was weakened, when the immigrants became assimilated into their new country.

International trade is also a branch of economics, which, together with international finance, forms the larger branch of international economics. Trading is a value added function of the economic process of a product finding its market, where specific risks are to be borne by the trader, affecting the assets being traded which will be mitigated by performing specific functions.

Fundamentals of Trade

Supply and Demand determine price. As supply goes up, price goes down. As demand goes up, price goes up (if supply remains constant).

Increased prices imply higher profits. Higher profits generally motivate other competitors to provide the same good. Supply goes up, prices go down. If prices go down enough, competitors will go out of business, and supply will go down. Prices will begin to rise. In the end, there tends to be enough supply, and enough suppliers, to meet demand at prices that guarantee some but not overly high profits. This magical equilibrium is Adam Smith's Invisible Hand (invisible hands are one reason that economists are famous for and can get away with saying "on the one hand...).

This equilibrium is the cornerstone of faith in liberal economics. Liberal in economics means belief in free trade and unregulated markets.

Natural equilibrium of markets depends on two core assumptions. The first is that there are multiple suppliers. Lack of multiple suppliers erodes competition, raises prices, reduces efficiency, and is called oligopoly or monopoly. The second is that consumers have good information and can make informed decisions about products. Competition wouldn't work, if you didn't know the same thing was available for cheaper around the corner.

Largest countries by total international trade

Rank	Country	International Trade of Goods (Billions of USD)	Date of information
-	World	36,688.0	2012 est.
-	European Union	4,469.3	2012 est.
1	China	3,982.0	2013 est.
2	United States	3,848.0	2013 est.
3	Germany	2,726.0	2013 est.
4	Japan	1,463.6	2013 est.
5	France	1,210.2	2013 est.
6	United Kingdom	1,121.7	2013 est.
7	South Korea	1,073.9	2013 est.
8	Netherlands	1,028.8	2013 est.
9	Hong Kong	1,000.6	2013 est.
10	Canada	929.7	2013 est.
11	Italy	909.8	2013 est.
12	Spain	889.0	2013 est.
13	Russia	856.0	2013 est.
14	**India**	**832.9**	**2013 est.**
15	Singapore	823.2	2013 est.
16	Mexico	741.6	2013 est.
17	United Arab Emirates	618.5	2013 est.
18	Belgium	605.5	2013 est.
19	Switzerland	588.0	2013 est.
20	Taiwan	574.3	2013 est.

Rank	Country	International Trade of Services (Billions of USD)	Date of information
-	World	8,452.6	2012 est.
-	European Union	1,465.8	2012 est.
1	United States	1,019.7	2012 est.
2	Germany	539.7	2012 est.
3	China	471.0	2012 est.
4	United Kingdom	453.9	2012 est.
5	France	379.2	2012 est.
6	Japan	313.4	2012 est.
7	Pakistan	272.8	2012 est.
8	Singapore	250.1	2012 est.
9	Spain	229.3	2012 est.
10	South Korea	214.2	2012 est.

Top traded commodities (exports)

Rank	Commodity	Value in US$('000)	Date of information
1	Mineral fuels, oils, distillation products, etc.	$2,183,079,941	2012
2	Electrical, electronic equipment	$1,833,534,414	2012
3	Machinery, nuclear reactors, boilers, etc.	$1,763,371,813	2012
4	Vehicles other than railway	$1,076,830,856	2012
5	Plastics and articles thereof	$470,226,676	2012
6	Optical, photo, technical, medical, etc. apparatus	$465,101,524	2012
7	Pharmaceutical products	$443,596,577	2012
8	Iron and steel	$379,113,147	2012
9	Organic chemicals	$377,462,088	2012
10	Pearls, precious stones, metals, coins, etc.	$348,155,369	2012

Source: International Trade Centre

❐❐❐

Chapter 8

World Trade Oraganization (WTO) and International Tropical Timber Organization (ITTO)

(**Formation** : 1 January, 1995, **HQ:** Geneva, Switzerland, **Membership**: 159 member states. **Official languages**: English, French, Spanish, **Director-General:** Roberto Azevêdo, **Budget**: 196 million Swiss francs (approx. 209 million US$) in 2011, **Staff:** 640, **Website**: wto.org.)

Introduction

WTO on April 15, 1994, a basis for a new world institution, world trade organization (WTO) laid. It has replaced general agreement on trade and tariffs (GATT). In respect of international trade and trade related matters which were made by Arther Daunkel (Director-General of GATT). The report is also known as Daunkel Draft.

The **General Agreement on Tariffs and Trade** (**GATT**) was a multi-lateral agreement regulating international trade. According to its preamble, its purpose was the "substantial reduction of tariffs and other trade barriers and the elimination of preferences, on a reciprocal and mutually advantageous basis." It was negotiated during the United Nations Conference on Trade and Employment and was the outcome of the failure of negotiating governments to create the International Trade Organization (ITO). **GATT was signed in 1947 and lasted until 1994, when it was replaced by the World Trade Organization in 1st Jan, 1995.**

Objectives and Provisions

1. The GATT is comprised of a trade pact among the members' countries and organization

2. It is a basically forum for international bargaining on lowering the barriers to trade to libaralise it as among countries
3. It has evolved a set of rules for the conduct of world trade
4. The basic aim of the GATT has been to make international trade free from all barriers
5. GATT is an instrument in rapid expansion of international trade
6. Trade has also expanded vastly through the promotion of multinational trading system, under the agreement of GATT. This system allows balancing of trade through a third country
7. GATT which facilitated rapid expansion of trade is the Most Favoured Nations (MFN) treatment under it, any concision given to member countries of GATT
8. GATT has also provided on effective mechanism for settlement of disputes among the trading countries
9. Improving the balance of payments.

Short Comings of GATT (Disadvantages)

1. Losing a comparative advantage
2. Insufficient provision for agriculture subsidies
3. Inadequate provision for the small farmers and the poor
4. Inappropriateness of patenting living organism
5. Unequal competition
6. No provision for small scale industries or cottage based industries.

World Trade Organization's Threat to Forest Protection

The World Trade Organization ("WTO") - the international institution at promotes free trade - is at a crossroads. In Seattle on November 1999, it was decided on the agenda for a new round of negotiations. The world's forests are likely to be on the chopping block. The WTO threatens to fuel the destruction of the world's remaining forests. This threat arises out of existing WTO rules, and a proposed "global free logging agreement" that would expand those rules.

1. Invasive Species Safeguards

Invasive species are the second leading threat to forest biodiversity. The most effective way to prevent bio invasions of forests is to prevent the entry and spread of invasive species. Yet a ban or other restrictions on imports of wood products apt to harbour invasive pests would collide with restrictive **WTO** rules that require that regulations be based on definitive proof of a risk from each country, and that they use the least trade restrictive means of achieving the regulatory goal.

2. Raw Log Export Bans

In the face of unsustainable logging rates, the United States and states in the western United States have banned the export of unprocessed (raw) logs from public lands. Such export bans reduce the demand for logging and enable domestic mills to reap the benefits of logging that is done. WTO rules prohibit such export bans.

3. Green Procurement

Through green procurement, governments use their purchasing power to decrease consumption of products from native and unsustainably managed forests and to increase demand for and use of recycled paper. Recycled content requirements are firmly in place for federal, state, and local government procurement. Under WTO rules, such rules are vulnerable to challenge on the ground that they discriminate against countries that log native forests. Government procurement preferences for products from sustainably managed forests, under consideration by many local governments, run a foul of WTO rules that prohibit different treatment of products, based on the way the product is produced.

4. Eco-labelling and Forest Certification

Eco-labelling enables consumers to identify and purchase environmentally friendly products. Forest certification schemes disclose whether forest products have been produced in a sustainable and environmentally sound manner. Many forests throughout the west have obtained such certifications. WTO rules create obstacles for such "lifecycle" eco-labelling because it is based on how the product is produced, not simply on the product's characteristics.

5. Trade Liberalization without Environmental Safeguards

The United States is leading the charge to further liberalize trade in forest products. It is currently spearheading negotiations to eliminate tariffs on forest products with the goal of reaching a worldwide tariff agreement by the Ministerial that will begin in Seattle on November 30, 1999. If the WTO succeeds in increasing trade in forest products, the rate of deforestation will increase. However, nothing in the WTO rules requires or seeks to ensure that the logging will be done in a sustainable manner, or that forest resources be subject to environmental safeguards. The elimination of national, state, and local protections will result in a void, leading to mounting deforestation and degradation of the world's forests.

6. Some "barriers" that have been targeted for expanded trade constraints

- Border safeguards to prevent the entry and spread of invasive species that could wreak havoc in forest ecosystems.
- Government procurement preferences for recycled paper or products from sustainably managed forests.
- Eco-labelling that tells consumers whether wood products were produced sustainably and without harm to the environment.
- Environmental laws that protect forests but impose restrictions on how foreign investors may run their investments. New investor rights threaten to thwart forest protections because they seek money damages from governments that restrict their investments, even if through environmental regulations. Many of these forest protections are under consideration for the new round of WTO negotiations.
- The WTO should review and repair the damage its rules cause to forests before expanding. The WTO's threat is magnified by what is not on the table.
- Trade negotiations are focusing on removing trade barriers, not on protecting forests. The WTO does not develop solutions to environmental threats. The WTO is not deferring to governments or international institutions that are developing forest protection strategies that respond to scientific evidence and political demands. Instead, the WTO is reaching out worldwide to prohibit a vast array of forest protections, without putting other protections into place.

- This one-sided rush to establish trade promotion rules that displace forest protections is untenable. Governments have historically had control over the natural resources within their borders. They should retain full authority to protect their forests. The world's forests should not be on a WTO chopping block.
- The WTO's accelerated push to negotiate a global free logging agreement puts the cart before the horse. Environmentalist groups have demanded, it is time to slow down and take stock of the threat that the existing WTO rules pose before increasing their reach and severity.
- The WTO should review its rules to assess the extent to which they stand in the way of sustainable forest practices that protect native forest habitats. The WTO should then repair the damage its unbalanced rules and biased processes threaten to cause to world forests.

World Trade Organization

Background, Structure, Functions and Decision-Making Process

Formation	:	1 January, 1995
Headquarters	:	Centre William Rappard, Geneva, Switzerland
Membership	:	164 member states
Official languages	:	English, French, Spanish
Director-General	:	Roberto Azevêdo
Budget	:	197 million Swiss francs (approx. 209 million US$) in 2012.
Staff	:	640
Website	:	wto.org

The World Trade Organization (WTO) is an organization that intends to supervise and liberalize international trade. The organization officially commenced on 1 January, 1995 under the Marrakech Agreement, replacing the General Agreement on Tariffs and Trade (GATT), which commenced in 1948. The organization deals with regulation of trade between participating countries; it provides a framework for negotiating and formalizing trade agreements, and a dispute resolution process aimed at enforcing participant's adherence to WTO agreements, which are signed by representatives of member governments and ratified by their parliaments. Most of the issues that the WTO focuses on derive from previous trade negotiations, especially from the Uruguay Round (1986–1994).

The organization is attempting to complete negotiations on the Doha Development Round, which was launched in 2001 with an explicit focus on addressing the needs of developing countries. As of June, 2012, the future of the Doha Round remained uncertain: the work programme lists 21 subjects in which the original deadline of 1 January, 2005 was missed, and the round is still incomplete. The conflict between free trade on industrial goods and services but retention of protectionism on farm subsidies to domestic agricultural sector (requested by developed countries) and the substantiation of the international liberalization of fair trade on agricultural products (requested by developing countries) remain the major obstacles. These points of contention have hindered any progress to launch new WTO negotiations beyond the Doha Development Round. As a result of this impasse, there have been an increasing number of bilateral free trade agreements signed. As of July 2012, there were various negotiation groups in the WTO system for the current agricultural trade negotiation, which is in the condition of stalemate.

WTO's current Director-General is Roberto Azevêdo, who leads a staff of over 600 people in Geneva, Switzerland. A trade facilitation agreement known as the Bali Package was reached by all members on 7 December, 2013, the first comprehensive agreement in the organization's history.

History

The economists Harry White (left) and John Maynard Keynes at the Bretton Woods Conference. Both had been strong advocates of a central-controlled international trade environment and recommended the establishment of three institutions: the IMF (for fiscal and monetary issues); the World Bank (for financial and structural issues); and the ITO (for international economic co-operation).

The WTO's predecessor, the General Agreement on Tariffs and Trade (GATT), was established after World War II in the wake of other new multilateral institutions dedicated to international economic co-operation - notably the Bretton Woods institutions known as the World Bank and the International Monetary Fund (IMF). A comparable international institution for trade, named the International

Trade Organization was successfully negotiated. The ITO was to be a United Nations specialized agency and would address not only trade barriers but also other issues indirectly related to trade, including employment, investment, restrictive business practices, and commodity agreements. But the ITO treaty was not approved by the U.S. and a few other signatories and never went into effect.

In the absence of an international organization for trade, the GATT would over the years "transform itself" into a *de facto* international organization.

GATT rounds of negotiations

The GATT was the only multilateral instrument governing international trade from 1946 until the WTO was established on 1 January, 1995. Despite attempts in the mid-1950s and 1960s to create some form of institutional mechanism for international trade, the GATT continued to operate for almost half a century as a semi-institutionalized multilateral treaty regime on a provisional basis.

From Geneva to Tokyo

Seven rounds of negotiations occurred under GATT. The first real GATT trade rounds concentrated on further reducing tariffs. Then, the Kennedy Round in the mid-sixties brought about a GATT anti-dumping Agreement and a section on development. The Tokyo Round during the seventies was the first major attempt to tackle trade barriers that do not take the form of tariffs, and to improve the system, adopting a series of agreements on non-tariff barriers, which in some cases interpreted existing GATT rules, and in others broke entirely new ground. Because these plurilateral agreements were not accepted by the full GATT membership, they were often informally called "codes". Several of these codes were amended in the Uruguay Round, and turned into multilateral commitments, accepted by all WTO members. Only four remained plurilateral (those on government procurement, bovine meat, civil aircraft and dairy products), but in 1997 WTO members agreed to terminate the bovine meat and dairy agreements, leaving only two.

Uruguay Round

During the Doha Round, the US government blamed Brazil and India for being inflexible and the EU for impeding agricultural imports. The then-President of Brazil, Luiz Inácio Lula da Silva (above right), responded to the criticisms by arguing that progress would only be achieved, if the richest countries (especially the US and countries in the EU) made deeper cuts in agricultural subsidies and further opened their markets for agricultural goods.

Well before GATT's 40th anniversary, its members concluded that the GATT system was straining to adapt to a new globalizing world economy. In response to the problems identified in the 1982 Ministerial Declaration (structural deficiencies, spill-over impacts of certain countries' policies on world trade GATT could not manage, etc.), the eighth GATT round - known as the Uruguay Round - was launched in September 1986, in Punta del Este, Uruguay.

It was the biggest negotiating mandate on trade ever agreed: the talks were going to extend the trading system into several new areas, notably trade in services and intellectual property, and to reform trade in the sensitive sectors of agriculture and textiles; all the original GATT articles were up for review. The Final Act concluding the Uruguay Round and officially establishing the WTO regime was signed 15 April, 1994, during the ministerial meeting at Marrakesh, Morocco, and hence, is known as the Marrakesh Agreement.

The GATT still exists as the WTO's umbrella treaty for trade in goods, updated as a result of the Uruguay Round negotiations (a distinction is made between *GATT, 1994*, the updated parts of GATT, and *GATT, 1947*, the original agreement which is still the heart of GATT, 1994). GATT, 1994 is not 'however' the only legally binding agreement included via the Final Act at Marrakesh; a long list of about 60 agreements, annexes, decisions and understandings was adopted.

The agreements fall into a structure with six main parts :

- The Agreement Establishing the WTO
- Goods and investment - the Multilateral Agreements on Trade in Goods including the GATT, 1994 and the Trade Related Investment Measures (TRIMS)
- Services — the General Agreement on Trade in Services

- Intellectual property – the Agreement on Trade-Related Aspects of Intellectual Property Rights (TRIPS)
- Dispute settlement (DSU)
- Reviews of governments' trade policies (TPRM)

In terms of the WTO's principle relating to tariff "ceiling-binding" (No. 3), the Uruguay Round has been successful in increasing binding commitments by both developed and developing countries, as may be seen in the percentages of tariffs bound before and after the 1986–1994 talks.

Ministerial conferences

The highest decision-making body of the WTO is the Ministerial Conference, which usually meets every two years. It brings together all members of the WTO, all of which are countries or customs unions. The Ministerial Conference can take decisions on all matters under any of the multilateral trade agreements. The inaugural ministerial conference was held in Singapore in 1996. Disagreements between largely developed and developing economies emerged during this conference over four issues initiated by this conference, which led to them being collectively referred to as the "Singapore issues". The second ministerial conference was held in Geneva in Switzerland. The third conference in Seattle, Washington ended in failure, with massive demonstrations and police and National Guard crowd-control efforts drawing worldwide attention. The fourth ministerial conference was held in Doha, in the Persian Gulf nation of Qatar. The Doha Development Round was launched at the conference. The conference also approved the joining of China, which became the 143rd member to join. The fifth ministerial conference was held in Cancún, Mexico, aiming at forging agreement on the Doha round. An alliance of 22 southern states, the G20 developing nations (led by India, China, Brazil, ASEAN led by the Philippines), resisted demands from the North for agreements on the so-called "Singapore issues" and called for an end to agricultural subsidies within the EU and the US. The talks broke down without progress.

The sixth WTO ministerial conference was held in Hong Kong from 13–18 December, 2005. It was considered vital, if the four-years-old Doha Development Round negotiations were to move forward sufficiently to conclude the round in 2006. In this meeting, countries agreed to phase out all their agricultural export subsidies by the end of 2013, and terminate any cotton export subsidies by the end of 2006. Further concessions to developing countries included an agreement to introduce duty-free, tariff-free access for goods from the Least Developed Countries, following the Everything but Arms initiative of the European Union-but with upto 3% of tariff lines exempted. Other major issues were left for further negotiation to be completed by the end of 2010. The WTO General Council, on 26 May, 2009, agreed to hold a seventh WTO ministerial conference session in Geneva from 30 November-3 December, 2009. A statement by chairman Amb. Mario Matus acknowledged that the prime purpose was to remedy a breach of protocol requiring two-yearly "regular" meetings, which had lapsed with the Doha Round failure in 2005, and that the "scaled-down" meeting would not be a negotiating session, but "emphasis will be on transparency and open discussion rather than on small group processes and informal negotiating structures". The general theme for discussion was "The WTO, the Multilateral Trading System and the Current Global Economic Environment".

Doha Round (Doha Agenda)

The WTO launched the current round of negotiations, the Doha Development Round, at the fourth ministerial conference in Doha, Qatar in November 2001. This was to be an ambitious effort to make globalization more inclusive and help the world's poor, particularly by slashing barriers and subsidies in farming. The initial agenda comprised both further trade liberalization and new rule-making, underpinned by commitments to strengthen substantial assistance to developing countries.

The negotiations have been highly contentious. Disagreements still continue over several key areas including agriculture subsidies, which emerged as critical in July 2006. According to a European Union statement, "The 2008 Ministerial meeting broke down over a disagreement between exporters of agricultural bulk commodities and countries with large numbers of subsistence farmers on the precise terms of a 'special safeguard measure' to protect farmers from surges in imports." The position of the European Commission is that "The successful conclusion of the Doha negotiations would confirm the central role of multilateral liberalisation and rule-making. It would confirm the WTO as a powerful shield against protectionist backsliding." An impasse remains and, as of August 2013, agreement has not been reached, despite intense negotiations at several ministerial conferences and at other sessions. On 27 March, 2013, the chairman of agriculture talks announced "a proposal to loosen price support disciplines for developing countries' public stocks and domestic food aid." He added: "...we are not yet close to agreement—in fact, the substantive discussion of the proposal is only beginning."

Functions

Among the various functions of the WTO, these are regarded by analysts as the most important:

- It oversees the implementation, administration and operation of the covered agreements.
- It provides a forum for negotiations and for settling disputes.

Additionally, it is the WTO's duty to review and propagate the national trade policies, and to ensure the coherence and transparency of trade policies through surveillance in global economic policy-making. Another priority of the WTO is the assistance of developing, least-developed and low-income countries in transition to adjust to WTO rules and disciplines through technical co-operation and training.

The WTO is also a centre of economic research and analysis: regular assessments of the global trade picture in its annual publications and research reports on specific topics are produced by the organization. Finally, the WTO cooperates closely with the two other components of the Bretton Woods system, the IMF and the World Bank.

Principles of the trading system

The WTO establishes a framework for trade policies; it does not define or specify outcomes. That is, it is concerned with setting the rules of the trade policy games. Five principles are of particular importance in understanding both the pre-1994 GATT and the WTO:

1. Non-discrimination: It has two major components: the most favoured nation (MFN) rule, and the national treatment policy. Both are embedded in the main WTO rules on goods, services, and intellectual property, but their precise scope and nature differ across these areas. The MFN rule requires that a WTO member must apply the same conditions on all trade with other WTO

members, i.e. a WTO member has to grant the most favourable conditions under which it allows trade in a certain product type to all other WTO members. "Grant someone a special favour and you have to do the same for all other WTO members." National treatment means that imported goods should be treated no less favourably than domestically produced goods (at least after the foreign goods have entered the market) and was introduced to tackle non-tariff barriers to trade (e.g. technical standards, security standards *et al.* discriminating against imported goods).

2. Reciprocity: It reflects both a desire to limit the scope of free-riding that may arise because of the MFN rule, and a desire to obtain better access to foreign markets. A related point is that for a nation to negotiate, it is necessary that the gain from doing so be greater than the gain available from unilateral liberalization; reciprocal concessions intend to ensure that such gains will materialize.
3. Binding and enforceable commitments: The tariff commitments made by WTO members in a multilateral trade negotiation and on accession are enumerated in a schedule (list) of concessions. These schedules establish "ceiling bindings": a country can change its bindings, but only after negotiating with its trading partners, which could mean compensating them for loss of trade. If satisfaction is not obtained, the complaining country may invoke the WTO dispute settlement procedures.
4. Transparency: The WTO members are required to publish their trade regulations, to maintain institutions allowing for the review of administrative decisions affecting trade, to respond to requests for information by other members, and to notify changes in trade policies to the WTO. These internal transparency requirements are supplemented and facilitated by periodic country-specific reports (trade policy reviews) through the Trade Policy Review Mechanism (TPRM). The WTO system tries also to improve predictability and stability, discouraging the use of quotas and other measures used to set limits on quantities of imports.
5. Safety valves: In specific circumstances, governments are able to restrict trade. The WTO's agreements permit members to take measures to protect not only the environment but also public health, animal health and plant health.

There are three types of provision in this direction:

- Articles allowing for the use of trade measures to attain non-economic objectives;
- Articles aimed at ensuring "fair competition"; members must not use environmental protection measures as a means of disguising protectionist policies;
- Provisions permitting intervention in trade for economic reasons.

Exceptions to the MFN principle also allow for preferential treatment of developing countries, regional free trade areas and customs unions.

Organizational structure

The General Council has the following subsidiary bodies, which oversee committees in different areas:

Council for Trade in Goods

There are 11 committees under the jurisdiction of the Goods Council each with a specific task. All members of the WTO participate in the committees. The Textiles Monitoring Body is separate from the other committees but still under the jurisdiction of Goods Council. The body has its own chairman and only 10 members. The body also has several groups relating to textiles.

Council for Trade-Related Aspects of Intellectual Property Rights

Information on intellectual property in the WTO, news and official records of the activities of the TRIPS Council, and details of the WTO's work with other international organizations in the field.[49]

Council for Trade in Services

The Council for Trade in Services operates under the guidance of the General Council and is responsible for overseeing the functioning of the General Agreement on Trade in Services (GATS). It is open to all WTO members, and can create subsidiary bodies, as required.

Trade Negotiations Committee

The Trade Negotiations Committee (TNC) is the committee that deals with the current trade talks round. The chair is WTO's director-general. As of June 2012, the committee was tasked with the Doha Development Round.

The Service Council has three subsidiary bodies: financial services, domestic regulations, GATS rules and specific commitments. The council has several different committees, working groups, and working parties. There are committees on the following: Trade and Environment; Trade and Development (Subcommittee on Least-Developed Countries); Regional Trade Agreements; Balance of Payments Restrictions; and Budget, Finance and Administration. There are working parties on the following: Accession. There are working groups on the following: Trade, debt and finance; and Trade and technology transfer.

Decision-making

The WTO describes itself as "a rules-based, member-driven organization-all decisions are made by the member governments, and the rules are the outcome of negotiations among members". The WTO Agreement foresees votes where consensus cannot be reached, but the practice of consensus dominates the process of decision-making.

Richard Harold Steinberg (2002) argues that although the WTO's consensus governance model provides law-based initial bargaining, trading rounds close through power-based bargaining favouring Europe and the U.S., and may not lead to Pareto improvement.

Dispute settlement

In 1994, the WTO members agreed on the Understanding on Rules and Procedures Governing the Settlement of Disputes (DSU) annexed to the "Final Act" signed in Marrakesh in 1994. Dispute settlement is regarded by the WTO as the central pillar of the multilateral trading system, and as a "unique contribution to the stability of the global economy". WTO members have agreed that, if they believe fellow-members are violating trade rules, they will use the multilateral system of settling disputes instead of taking action unilaterally.

The operation of the WTO dispute settlement process involves the DSB panels, the Appellate Body, the WTO Secretariat, arbitrators, independent experts and several specialized institutions. Bodies involved in the dispute settlement process, World Trade Organization.

Accession and membership

The process of becoming a WTO member is unique to each applicant country, and the terms of accession are dependent upon the country's stage of economic development and current trade regime. The process takes about five years, on average, but it can last more, if the country is less than fully committed to the process or if political issues interfere. The shortest accession negotiation was that of the Kyrgyz Republic, while the longest was that of Russia, which, having first applied to join GATT in 1993, was approved for membership in December 2011 and became a WTO member on 22 August, 2012. The second longest was that of Vanuatu, whose Working Party on the Accession of Vanuatu was established on 11 July, 1995. After a final meeting of the Working Party in October 2001, Vanuatu requested more time to consider its accession terms. In 2008, it indicated its interest to resume and conclude its WTO accession. The Working Party on the Accession of Vanuatu was reconvened informally on 4 April, 2011 to discuss Vanuatu's future WTO membership. The re-convened Working Party completed its mandate on 2 May, 2011. The General Council formally approved the Accession Package of Vanuatu on 26 October, 2011. On 24 August, 2012, the WTO welcomed Vanuatu as its 157th member. An offer of accession is only given once consensus is reached among interested parties.

Accession process

A country wishing to accede to the WTO submits an application to the General Council, and has to describe all aspects of its trade and economic policies that have a bearing on WTO agreements. The application is submitted to the WTO in a memorandum, which is examined by a working party open to all interested WTO Members.

After all necessary background information has been acquired, the working party focuses on issues of discrepancy between the WTO rules and the applicant's international and domestic trade policies and laws. The working party determines the terms and conditions of entry into the WTO for the applicant nation, and may consider transitional periods to allow countries some leeway in complying with the WTO rules. The final phase of accession involves bilateral negotiations between the applicant nation and other working party members regarding the concessions and commitments on tariff levels and market access for goods and services. The new member's commitments are to apply equally to all WTO members under normal non-discrimination rules, even though they are negotiated bilaterally.

When the bilateral talks conclude, the working party sends to the general council or ministerial conference an accession package, which includes a summary of all the working party meetings, the Protocol of Accession (a draft membership treaty), and lists ("schedules") of the member-to-be's commitments. Once the general council or ministerial conference approves of the terms of accession, the applicant's parliament must ratify the Protocol of Accession before it can become a member. Some countries may have faced tougher and a much longer accession process due to challenges during negotiations with other WTO members, such as Vietnam, whose negotiations took more than 11 years, before it became official member in January 2007.

Members and observers

The WTO has 159 members and 25 observer governments. In addition to states, the European Union is a member. WTO members do not have to be full sovereign nation-members. Instead, they must be a customs territory with full autonomy in the conduct of their external commercial relations. Thus, Hong Kong has been a member since 1995 (as "Hong Kong, China" since 1997) predating the People's Republic of China, which joined in 2001 after 15 years of negotiations. The Republic of China acceded to the WTO in 2002 as "Separate Customs Territory of Taiwan, Penghu, Kinmen and Matsu" (Chinese Taipei) despite its disputed status. The WTO Secretariat omits the official titles (such as Counsellor, First Secretary, Second Secretary and Third Secretary) of the members of Chinese Taipei's Permanent Mission to the WTO, except for the titles of the Permanent Representative and the Deputy Permanent Representative.

As of 2007, WTO member states represented 96.4% of global trade and 96.7% of global GDP.[71] Iran, followed by Algeria, are the economies with the largest GDP and trade outside the WTO, using 2005 data. With the exception of the Holy See, observers must start accession negotiations within five years of becoming observers.

A number of international inter-governmental organizations have also been granted observer status to WTO bodies. 14 states and two territories so far have no official interaction with the WTO.

Agreements

The WTO oversees about 60 different agreements which have the status of international legal texts. Member countries must sign and ratify all WTO agreements on accession.[75] A discussion of some of the most important agreements follows. The Agreement on Agriculture came into effect with the establishment of the WTO at the beginning of 1995. The AoA has three central concepts, or "pillars": domestic support, market access and export subsidies. The General Agreement on Trade in Services was created to extend the multilateral trading system to service sector, in the same way as the General Agreement on Tariffs and Trade (GATT) provided such a system for merchandise trade. The agreement entered into force in January 1995. The Agreement on Trade-Related Aspects of Intellectual Property Rights sets down minimum standards for many forms of intellectual property (IP) regulation. It was negotiated at the end of the Uruguay Round of the General Agreement on Tariffs and Trade (GATT) in 1994.

The Agreement on the Application of Sanitary and Phytosanitary Measures-also known as the SPS Agreement-was negotiated during the Uruguay Round of GATT, and entered into force with the establishment of the WTO at the beginning of 1995. Under the SPS agreement, the WTO sets constraints on members' policies relating to food safety (bacterial contaminants, pesticides, inspection and labelling) as well as animal and plant health (imported pests and diseases). The Agreement on Technical Barriers to Trade is an international treaty of the World Trade Organization. It was negotiated during the Uruguay Round of the General Agreement on Tariffs and Trade, and entered into force with the establishment of the WTO at the end of 1994. The object ensures that technical negotiations and standards, as well as testing and certification procedures, do not create unnecessary obstacles to trade".[77] The Agreement on Customs Valuation, formally known as the Agreement on Implementation of Article VII of GATT, prescribes methods of customs valuation that Members are to follow. Chiefly, it adopts the "transaction value" approach.

In December 2013, the biggest agreement within the WTO was signed and known as the Bali Package.

Office of Director-General

The headquarters of the World Trade Organization, in Geneva, Switzerland. The procedures for the appointment of the WTO director-general were published in January 2003. Additionally, there are four deputy directors-general. As of 1 October, 2013, under director-general Roberto Azevêdo, the four deputy directors-general are Yi Xiaozhun of China, Karl-Ernst Brauner of Germany, Yonov Frederick Agah of Nigeria and David Shark of the United States.

List of Directors-General

- Roberto Azevedo, 2013–till date
- Pascal Lamy, 2005–2013
- Supachai Panitchpakdi, 2002–2005
- Mike Moore, 1999–2002
- Renato Ruggiero, 1995–1999
- Peter Sutherland, 1995

(Heads of the precursor organization, GATT):

- Peter Sutherland, 1993–1995
- Arthur Dunkel, 1980–1993
- Olivier Long, 1968–1980
- Eric Wyndham White, 1948–1968

International Tropical Timber Organization (ITTO)

(ITTO established in 1986; Headquarter – Yokohama, Japan)

ITTO is an inter-governmental organization promoting the conservation and sustainable management, use and trade of tropical forest resources. Its members represent about 80% of the world's tropical forests and 90% of the global tropical timber trade.

The International Tropical Timber Organization (ITTO) was established under the auspices of the United Nations in 1986 amidst increasing worldwide concern for the fate of tropical forests. While almost everyone was alarmed at the rate of deforestation occurring in many tropical countries, there was also considerable agreement that the tropical timber trade was one of the keys to economic development in those same countries.

ITTO's origins can be traced back to 1976, when the long series of negotiations that led to the first International Tropical Timber Agreement (ITTA) began at the fourth session of the **United Nations Conference on Trade and Development (UNCTAD)** as part of that organization's Programme for Commodities. The eventual outcome of these negotiations was the ITTA, 1983, which governed the Organization's work until 31 December, 1996, when it was superseded by the ITTA, 1994. Negotiations for a successor to this agreement were concluded in 2006, again under the auspices of UNCTAD. The ITTA, 2006 entered into force on December 7, 2011.

A unique organization

ITTO occupies an unusual position in the family of intergovernmental organizations. Like all commodity organizations, it is concerned with trade and industry, but like an environmental agreement it also pays considerable attention to the sustainable management of natural resources. It manages its own program of projects and other activities, enabling it to quickly test and operationalize its policy work. Other features include:

- An equal partnership in decision-making, policy formulation and project development between producing members (tropical developing countries) and tropical timber consuming members (mostly temperate developed countries);
- The active participation of civil society and trade organizations in meetings and project work;
- The formulation and implementation of projects in producing member countries, using mostly local expertise;
- Frequent meetings of its governing body (the International Tropical Timber Council), meaning a comparatively rapid pace of debate, decisions and action.

What ITTO does?

ITTO develops internationally agreed policy documents to promote sustainable forest management and forest conservation and assists tropical member countries to adapt such policies to local circumstances and to implement them in the field through projects. In addition, ITTO collects, analyses and disseminates data on the production and trade of tropical timber and funds a range of projects and other action aimed at developing industries at both community and industrial scales. For more information on ITTO's action program go to ITTO at work, or see the Organization's Biennial Work Programme.

Members may submit project proposals to the Council for review and financing in accordance with the ITTO project cycle. Examples include pilot and demonstration projects, human resource development projects, and research and development projects; the Organization's Action Plan sets out the types of activities that it should undertake in project and policy work. All projects are funded by voluntary contributions, mostly from consuming member countries. Since it became operational in 1987, ITTO has funded more than 800 projects, pre-projects and activities valued at more than US$300 million. The major donors are the governments of Japan, Switzerland, the USA, the Netherlands and the EU.

ITTO's structure

The governing body of the ITTO is the International Tropical Timber Council, which is composed of all the Organization's members. ITTO has two categories of membership: producing and consuming. Annual contributions and votes are distributed equally between these two groups, which are called caucuses. Within each caucus, the dues and votes of individual members are calculated based on tropical timber trade and, in the case of producers, also on the extent of tropical forests within the country.

The Council is supported by four committees, which are open to all members and observers and provide advice and assistance to the Council on policy and project issues. Three of the committees deal with key areas of policy and project work: economic information and market intelligence; re-forestation and forest management; and forest industry. These committees are supported by the Expert Panel for the Technical Appraisal of Projects and Pre-projects, which reviews project proposals for technical merit and relevance to ITTO objectives. The fourth committee, on Finance and Administration, advises the Council on matters related to the budget and other funding and administrative issues concerning the management of the Organization. ITTO's organizational structure is shown graphically in its current Action Plan.

Non-member stakeholders have established two advisory groups to facilitate their participation in the Council and to provide input to the Council's decision-making process. These are the Trade Advisory Group (TAG) and the Civil Society Advisory Group (CSAG).

ITTO's small secretariat of about 35 staff is based in Yokohama, Japan. It is headed by an Executive Director, who is responsible to the Council for the administration and operation of the Agreement in accordance with decisions made by the Council. The Organization also has regional officers in Latin America and Africa to assist with project monitoring and other duties.

National Bank for Agriculture and Rural Development (NABARD)

Headquarters : Mumbai, Maharashtra, India

Established : 12 July, 1982[1]

Chairman : Dr. Harsh Kumar Bhanwala

Currency : (Rupees)

Reserves : Rs. 81,220 crore (2007)

Website : www.nabard.org

NABARD is the apex development bank in India

National Bank for Agriculture and Rural Development (NABARD) is an apex development bank in India having headquarters based in Mumbai (Maharashtra) and other branches are all over the country. The Committee to Review Arrangements for Institutional Credit for Agriculture and Rural Development (CRAFICARD), set up by the Reserve Bank of India (RBI), under the Chairmanship of Shri B. Sivaraman, conceived and recommended the establishment of the National Bank for Agriculture and Rural Development (NABARD). It was established on 12 July, 1982 by a special Act by the parliament and its main focus was to uplift rural India by increasing the credit flow for elevation of agriculture & rural non-farm sector and completed its 25 years on 12 July, 2007. It has been accredited with "matters concerning policy, planning and operations in the field of credit for agriculture and other economic activities in rural areas in India". RBI sold its stake in NABARD to the Government of India, which now holds 99% stake. NABARD is active in developing financial inclusion policy and is a member of the Alliance for Financial Inclusion.

History

NABARD was established on the recommendations of Shivaraman Committee, (by Act 61, 1981 of Parliament) on 12 July, 1982 to implement the *National Bank for Agriculture and Rural Development Act, 1981*. It replaced the Agricultural Credit Department (ACD) and Rural Planning and Credit Cell (RPCC) of Reserve Bank of India, and Agricultural Refinance and Development Corporation (ARDC). It is one of the premier agencies to provide credit in rural areas. Nabard is India's specialised bank.

Associated with NABARD

International associates of NABARD ranges from World Bank-affiliated organizations to global developmental agencies working in the field of agriculture and rural development. These organizations help NABARD by advising and giving monetary aid for the upliftment of the people in the rural areas and optimizing the agricultural process.

Role

NABARD is the apex institution in the country which looks after the development of the cottage industry, small industry and village industry, and other rural industries. NABARD also reaches out to allied economies and supports and promotes integrated development. And to help NABARD discharge its duty, it has been given certain roles as follows:

1. Serves as an apex financing agency for the institutions providing investment and production credit for promoting the various developmental activities in rural areas
2. Takes measures towards institution building for improving absorptive capacity of the credit delivery system, including monitoring, formulation of rehabilitation schemes, restructuring of credit institutions, training of personnel, etc.

3. Co-ordinates the rural financing activities of all institutions engaged in developmental work at the field level and maintains liaison with Government of India, State Governments, Reserve Bank of India (RBI) and other national level institutions concerned with policy formulation
4. Undertakes monitoring and evaluation of projects refinanced by it.
5. NABARD refinances the financial institutions which finances the rural sector.
6. The institutions which help the rural economy, NABARD helps develop.
7. NABARD also keeps a check on its client institutes.
8. It regulates the institution which provides financial help to the rural economy.
9. It provides training facilities to the institutions working the field of rural upliftment.
10. It regulates the co-operative banks and the RRB's, and manages talent acquisition through IBPS CWE.

NABARD's refinance is available to State Co-operative Agriculture and Rural Development Banks (SCARDBs), State Co-operative Banks (SCBs), Regional Rural Banks (RRBs), Commercial Banks (CBs) and other financial institutions approved by RBI. While the ultimate beneficiaries of investment credit can be individuals, partnership concerns, companies, State-owned corporations or co-operative societies, production credit is generally given to individuals. NABARD has its head office at Mumbai, India.

NABARD operates throughout the country through its 28 Regional Offices and one Sub-office, located in the capitals of all the states/union territories. Each Regional Office [RO] has a Chief General Manager [CGMs] as its head, and the Head office has several Top executives like the Executive Directors[ED], Managing Directors[MD], and the Chairperson.It has 336 District Offices across the country, one Sub-office at [[Port Blair]] and one special cell at Srinagar. It also has 6 training establishments.

NABARD is also known for its 'SHG Bank Linkage Programme' which encourages India's banks to lend to [[self-help group (finance)|self-help groups]] (SHGs). Because SHGs are composed mainly of poor women, this has evolved into an important Indian tool for microfinance. As of March 2006, 22 lakh SHGs representing 3.3 crore members had to been linked to credit through this programme.

NABARD also has a portfolio of Natural Resource Management Programmes involving diverse fields like Watershed Development, Tribal Development and Farm Innovation through dedicated funds set up for the purpose.

Rural innovation

NABARD role in rural development in India is phenomenal. National Bank For Agriculture & Rural Development (NABARD) is set up as an apex Development Bank by the Government of India with a mandate for facilitating credit flow for promotion and development of agriculture, cottage and village industries. The credit flow to agriculture activities sanctioned by NABARD reached Rs 1,57,480 crore in 2005-2006. The overall GDP is estimated to grow at 8.4 per cent. The Indian economy as a whole is poised for higher growth in the coming years. Role of NABARD in overall development of India in general and rural & agricultural in specific is highly pivotal.

Through assistance of Swiss Agency for Development and Co-operation, NABARD set up the Rural Infrastructure Development Fund. Under the RIDF scheme Rs. 51,283 crore have been sanctioned for 2,44,651 projects covering irrigation, rural roads and bridges, health and education, soil conservation, water schemes, etc. Rural Innovation Fund is a fund designed to support innovative, risk friendly, unconventional experiments in these sectors that would have the potential to promote livelihood opportunities and employment in rural areas.[11] The assistance is extended to Individuals, NGOs, Cooperatives, Self Help Group, and Panchayati Raj Institutions, who have the expertise and willingness to implement innovative ideas for improving the quality of life in rural areas. Through member base of 25 crore, 6,00,000 co-operatives are working in India at grass root level in almost every sector of economy. There are linkages between SHG and other type institutes with that of co-operatives.

The purpose of RIDF is to promote innovation in rural & agricultural sector through viable means. Effectiveness of the program depends upon many factors, but the type of organization to which the assistance is extended is crucial one in generating, executing ideas in optimum commercial way. Co-operative is member driven formal organization for socio-economic purpose, while SHG is informal one. NGO have more of social colour while that of PRI is political one. Does the legal status of an institute influences effectiveness of the program? How & to what an extent? Co-operative type of organization is better (Financial efficiency & effectiveness) in functioning (agriculture & rural sector) compared to NGO, SHG & PRIs.

Recently in 2007-08, NABARD has started a new direct lending facility under 'Umbrella Programme for Natural Resource Management' (UPNRM). Under this facility financial support for natural resource management activities can be provided as a loan at reasonable rate of interest. Already 35 projects have been sanctioned involving loan amount of about Rs 1000 crore. The sanctioned projects include honey collection by tribals in Maharashtra, tussar value chain by a women producer company ('MASUTA'), eco-tourism in Karnataka, etc.

Microfinance and NABARD

Thus, the Reserve Bank of INDIA and NABARD has laid out certain guidelines in 06-07 for the commercial banks, Regional Rural Banks and Co-operative Banks to provide the data to RBI and its data regarding loans given by banks to the microfinance institutions.

NABARD a 100 % CSR company

NABARD has been instrumental in grounding rural,social innovations and social enterprises in the rural hinterlands. This endeavour is perhaps unparallelled in the country, it has in the process partnered with about 4000 partner organisations in grounding many of the interventions be it, SHG-Bank Linkage programme, tree-based tribal communities' livelihoods initiative, watershed approach in soil and water conservation, increasing crop productivity initiatives through lead crop initiative or dissemination of information flow to agrarian communities through Farmer clubs.Despite all this, it pays huge taxes too, to the exchequer-figuring in the top 50 tax-payers consistently. NABARD virtually ploughs back all the profits for development spending, in their unending search for solutions and answers. Thus, the organisation had developed a huge amount of trust capital in its 3 decades of work with rural communities.

Chapter 9

IPR's and their Implications for Forestry and Allied Sectors in India World Intellectual Property Organization (WIPO)

Intellectual Property Rights (IPR)

Introduction

Intellectual property rights as a collective term includes the following independent IP Rights, which can be collectively used for protecting different aspects of an inventive work for multiple protection:

- Patents
- Copyrights
- Trademarks
- Registered (industrial) design
- Protection of IC layout design
- Geographical indications
- Protection of undisclosed information

Nature of Intellectual Property Rights

IPR are largely territorial rights except copyright, which is global in nature in the sense that it is immediately available in all the members of the Berne Convention. These rights are awarded by the State and are monopoly rights implying that no one can use these rights without the consent of the right holder. It is important to know that these rights have to be renewed from time to time for keeping them in force except in case of copyright and trade secrets. IPR have fixed term except trademark and geographical indications, which can have indefinite life provided these are renewed after a stipulated time specified in the law by paying official fees. Trade secrets also have an infinite life but they don't have to be renewed. IPR can be assigned, gifted, sold and licensed like any other property. Unlike other moveable and immoveable properties, these rights can be simultaneously held in many countries at the same time. IPR can be held only by legal entities i.e., who have the right to sell and purchase property. In other words, an institution, which is not autonomous may not in a position to own an intellectual property. These rights especially patents, copyrights, industrial designs, IC layout design and trade secrets are associated with something new or original and therefore, what is known in public domain cannot be protected through the rights mentioned above. Improvements and modifications made over known things can be protected. It would, however, be possible to utilize geographical indications for protecting some agriculture and traditional products.

Patents

A patent is an exclusive right granted by a country to the owner of an invention to make, use, manufacture and market the invention, provided the invention satisfies certain conditions stipulated in the law. Exclusive right implies that no one else can make, use, manufacture or market the invention without the consent of the patent holder. This right is available for a limited period of time. In spite of the ownership of the rights, the use or exploitation of the rights by the owner of the patent may not be possible due to other laws of the country which has awarded the patent. These laws may relate to health, safety, food, security, etc. Further, existing patents in similar area may also come in the way. A patent in the law is a property right and hence, can be gifted, inherited, assigned, sold or licensed. As the right is conferred by the State, it can be revoked by the State under very special circumstances even if the patent has been sold or licensed or manufactured or marketed in the meantime. The patent right is territorial in nature and inventors/their assignees will have to file separate patent applications in countries of their 3 interest, along with necessary fees, for obtaining patents in those countries. A new chemical process or a drug molecule or an electronic circuit or a new surgical instrument or a vaccine is a patentable subject matter provided all the stipulations of the law are satisfied.

The Indian Patent Act

The first Indian patent laws were first promulgated in 1856. These were modified from time to time. New patent laws were made after the independence in the form of the Indian Patent Act, 1970. The Act has now been radically amended to become fully compliant with the provisions of TRIPS. The most recent amendments were made in 2005 which were preceded by the amendments in 2000 and 2003. While the process of bringing out amendments was going on, India became a member of the Paris Convention, Patent Cooperation Treaty and Budapest Treaty. The salient and important features of the amended Act are explained here.

Definition of invention

A clear definition has now been provided for an invention, which makes it at par with definitions, followed by most countries. Invention means a new product or process involving an inventive step and capable of industrial application. New invention means any invention or technology which has not been anticipated by publication in any document or used in the country or elsewhere in the world before the date of filing of patent application with complete specification i.e., the subject matter has not fallen in public domain or it does not form part of the state of the art. Inventive step means a feature of an invention that involves technical advance, as compared to existing knowledge or having economic significance or both and that makes the invention not obvious to a person skilled in the art. "Capable of industrial application means that the invention is capable of being made or used in an industry".

Novelty

An invention will be considered novel, if it does not form a part of the global state of the art. Information appearing in magazines, technical journals, books, newspapers, etc. constitute the state of the art. Oral description of the invention in a seminar/conference can also spoil novelty. Novelty is assessed in a global context. An invention will cease to be novel, if it has been disclosed in the public through any type of publications anywhere in the world before filing a patent application in respect of the invention. Therefore, it is advisable to file a patent application before publishing a paper, if there is a slight chance that the invention may be patentable. Prior use of the invention in the country of interest before the filing date can also destroy the novelty. Novelty is determined through extensive literature and patent searches. It should be realized that patent search is essential and critical for ascertaining novelty as most of the information reported in patent documents does not get published anywhere else. For an invention to be novel, it need not be a major breakthrough. No invention is small or big. Modifications to the existing state of the art, process or product or both, can also be candidates for patents, provided these were not for earlier known. In a chemical process, for example, use of new reactants, use of a catalyst, new process conditions can lead to a patentable invention.

Inventiveness (Non-obviousness)

A patent application involves an inventive step, if the proposed invention is not obvious to a person skilled in the art i.e., skilled in the subject matter of the patent application. The prior art should not point towards the invention implying that the practitioner of the subject matter could not have thought about the invention prior to filing of the patent application. Inventiveness cannot be decided on the material contained in unpublished patents. The complexity or the simplicity of an inventive step does not have any bearing on the grant of a patent. In other words, a very simple invention can qualify for a patent. If there is an inventive step between the proposed patent and the prior art at that point of time, then an invention has taken place. A mere 'scintilla' of invention is sufficient to found a valid patent. It may be often difficult to establish the inventiveness, especially in the area of up coming knowledge areas. The reason is that it would depend a great deal on the interpretative skills of the inventor and these skills will really be a function of knowledge in the subject area.

Usefulness

An invention must possess utility for the grant of patent. No valid patent can be granted for an invention devoid of utility. The patent specification should spell out various uses and manner of practicing them, even if considered obvious. If you are claiming a process, you need not describe the use of the compound produced thereby. Nevertheless, it would be safer to do so. But if you claim a compound without spelling out its utility, you may be denied a patent.

Copyrights

Copyright is a right, which is available for creating an original literary or dramatic or musical or artistic work. Cinematographic films including sound track and ideo films and recordings on discs, tapes, perforated roll or other devices are covered by copyrights. Computer programs and software are covered under literary works and are protected in India under copyrights. The Copyright Act, 1957 as amended in 1983, 1984, 1992, 1994 and 1999, governs the copyright protection in India. The total term of protection for literary work is the author's life plus sixty years. For cinematographic films, records, photographs, posthumous publications, anonymous publication, works of government and international agencies, the term is 60 years from the beginning of the calendar year, following the year in which the work was published. For broadcasting, the term is 25 years from the beginning of the calendar year, following the year in which the broadcast was made.

Trademarks

A trademark is a distinctive sign, which identifies certain goods or services as those produced or provided by a specific person or enterprise. Trademarks may be one or combination of words, letters, and numerals. They may also consist of drawings, symbols, three dimensional signs, such as shape and packaging of goods, or colours used as distinguishing feature. Collective marks are owned by an association whose members use them to identify themselves with a level of quality. Certification marks are given for compliance with defined standards. (Example ISO 9000.). A trademark provides to the owner of the mark by ensuring the exclusive right to use it to identify goods or services, or to authorize others to use it in return for some consideration (payment).

Industrial Design

We see so many varieties and brands of the same product (e.g. car, television, personal computer, a piece of furniture, etc.) in the market, which look quite different from each other. If the products have similar functional features or have comparable price tags, the eye appeal or visual design of a product determines the choice. Even if the similarities are not close, a person may decide to go for a more expensive item because that item has a better look or colour scheme.

What is being said is that the external design or colour scheme or ornamentation of a product plays a key role in determining the market acceptability of the product over other similar products. If you have a good design that gives you an advantage, then you must have a system to protect its features otherwise there would be wide scale imitation.

Protection of Geographical Indications

Indications which identify a good as originating in the territory of a member or a region or a locality in that territory, where a given quality reputation or other characteristics of the good is attributable to its geographical origin. The concept of identifying GI and protecting them is a new concept in India, perhaps in most developing countries, and has come to knowledge in these countries after they signed the TRIPS Agreement. It may be noted that properly protected GI will give protection in domestic and international market. Stipulations of TRIPS would be applicable to all the member countries. According to TRIPS, GI which is not or cease to be protected in its country of origin or which has fallen into disuse in that country cannot be protected. Homonymous GI for wines will get independent protection. Each state shall determine conditions under which homonymous indications will be differentiated from each other. Principles of national treatment and fair competition are applicable. TRIPS provide for seizure of goods bearing false indications of GI. TRIPS provide for refusal or invalidation of registration of a trademark, containing a GI with respect to goods not originating in the territory indicated. The Geographical Indication of Goods (Registration and Protection) Act came into being in 2000. (The Act is not implemented at the time of writing the article as the rules have not been notified).

Protection of Integrated Circuit Layout Design (IC)

It provides protection for semi-conductor IC layout designs. India has now in place Semi-conductor Integrated Circuits Layout Design Act, 2000 to give protection to IC layout design. Layout design includes a layout of transistors and other circuitry elements and includes lead wires connecting such elements and expressed in any manner in a semi-conductor IC. Semi-conductor IC is a product having transistors and other circuitry elements, which are inseparably formed on a semi-conductor material or an insulating material or inside the semi-conductor material and designed to perform an electronic circuitry function. The term of the registration is 10 years from the date of filing.

Protection of Undisclosed Information

The protected subject matter is information lawfully within the control of a natural person or legal person that is secret that has commercial value because it is secret and that has been subject to reasonable steps by the person lawfully in control of the information, to keep it secret. Secret is defined as "secret in the sense that it is not, as a body or in the precise configuration and assembly of its components known among or readily accessible to persons within the circles that normally deal with the kind of information in question." Undisclosed information, generally known as trade secret/ confidential information, includes formula, pattern, compilation, programme, device, method, technique or process. Protection of undisclosed information is least known to players of IPR and also least talked about, although it is perhaps the most important form of protection for industries, R&D institutions and other agencies dealing with IPRs. Protection of undisclosed information/trade secret is not really new to humanity; at every stage of development people have evolved methods to keep important information secret, commonly by restricting the knowledge to their family members. Laws relating to all forms of IPR are at different stages of implementation in India, but there is no separate and exclusive law for protecting undisclosed information/trade secret or confidential information. The Contract Act of 1872 would, however, cover many aspects of trade secrets.

Biodiversity Act- 2002

India enacted the Biodiversity Act, 2002 to ensure maintenance, sustenance and development of its biodiversity. The Act has specific provisions about ownership of intellectual property rights associated with exploitation of biodiversity. Industries have to have the prior informed consent of the National Biodiversity Authority before exploring the biodiversity in India. In the event of R&D based on exploitation of biodiversity and associated local knowledge, there is a provision for sharing of benefits of such work with the local community. No direct flow of funds is expected to the community. Instead the Union Government will reach the benefits through State Governments to the community.

The other Act having its influence over other Acts related to IPR is the Information technology Act, 2000 which looks at the security aspect of material being transacted on internet.

Protection through the Biological Diversity Act (2002) - Key Features

- To regulate access to biological resources (BR) of the country with the purpose of securing equitable share of benefits arising out of the use of BR and its associated knowledge.
- To conserve and sustainable use of BR.
- To respect and protect knowledge of local communities related to BR.
- To share the benefits with local people as conservers of BR and owner of knowledge and information relating to use of BR
- Conservation and development of areas of importance for biodiversity. MAPs constitutes a great deal of BR and its usages has been recognised by the Act. Even after developing IP by using the country's MAPs bio-resources through proper legal permission, one has also to take approval from the National Biodiversity Authority (NBA) for filling an application for any form of IPR. This provision will take care of benefit sharing that will emerge due to utilization of our BR.

Intellectual Property Rights (IPR) applicable for MAPs

Agriculture has become subject to IPR only after the creation of World Trade Organization (WTO) as a result of the General Agreement on Tariffs and Trade (GATT) Uruguay Round agreement. It was thought that Agreement on Agriculture (AoA) is the central focus of WTO negotiations, since agriculture is lifeline of development of most countries in the world. It plays a pivotal role in ensuring food security, providing livelihoods, generating foreign exchange and determining the allocation of natural resources (Murphy, 2003). However, dominant interest within the AoA circles around greater market access and increase in volume of commodity flows. Agreement on Trade-Related Intellectual Property Rights (TRIPs) is the outcome of WTO which has direct impact on farmers' livelihood, food security and economic development of the country. TRIPs provides mechanism for common protection and enforcement of IPR, such as copyrights, trademarks and patents and also to make rules intended to limit international trade in counterfeit goods. The agreement also recognised that there are no uniform standards in the protection and enforcement of IPR and also no multilateral framework of principles. Various legal protection mechanisms available under the TRIPs for MAPs that can be harnessed the benefit in country's interest.

Protection of Plant Varieties and Farmers' Right Act (2001)

It allows the registration of three types of plant varieties. These are farmers' variety, extant varieties and new varieties (Bala Ravi, 2004). Although, most of the MAPs that are in cultivation, are farmers' varieties and an instrument is available now to safeguard these varieties from piracy by registration. However, much benefit can not be achieved in MAPs by the farmers because rule states that all the extant varieties are to be registered within the three years from the date of enforcement of this Act. According to the Act, extant varieties include farmers' varieties also. Only possibility left now is to register the farmers' variety, as new variety since provision is available for the farmers also to register new varieties.

World Intellectual Property Organization (WIPO)

WIPO headquarters in Geneva

Abbreviation	:	WIPO, OMPI
Formation	:	July 14, 1967
Type	:	Specialized Agency
Legal status	:	Active
Headquarters	:	Geneva, Switzerland
Head	:	*Director-General of WIPO* Francis Gurry
Website	:	www.wipo.int

The World Intellectual Property Organization (WIPO) is one of the 17 specialized agencies of the United Nations. WIPO was created in 1967 "to encourage creative activity, to promote the protection of intellectual property throughout the world."

WIPO currently has 187 member states, administers 26 international treaties, and is headquartered in Geneva, Switzerland. The current Director-General of WIPO is Francis Gurry, who took office on October 1, 2008. 186 of the UN Members as well as the Holy See are Members of WIPO. Non-members are the states of Marshall Islands, Federated States of Micronesia, Nauru, Palau, Solomon Islands, South Sudan and Timor-Leste. Palestine has observer status.

History

The predecessor to WIPO was the BIRPI (*Bureaux Internationaux Réunis pour la Protection de la Propriété Intellectuelle*, French acronym for *United International Bureaux for the Protection of Intellectual Property*), which had been established in 1893 to administer the Berne Convention for the Protection of Literary and Artistic Works and the Paris Convention for the Protection of Industrial Property.

WIPO was formally created by the Convention Establishing the World Intellectual Property Organization, which entered into force on April 26, 1970. Under Article 3 of this Convention, WIPO seeks to "promote the protection of intellectual property throughout the world." WIPO became a specialized agency of the UN in 1974. The Agreement between the United Nations and the World Intellectual Property Organization notes in Article 1 that WIPO is responsible "for promoting creative intellectual activity and for facilitating the transfer of technology related to industrial property to the developing countries in order to accelerate economic, social and cultural development, subject to the competence and responsibilities of the United Nations and its organs, particularly the United Nations Conference on Trade and Development, the United Nations Development Programme and the United Nations Industrial Development Organization, as well as of the United Nations Educational, Scientific and Cultural Organization and of other agencies within the United Nations system."

The Agreement marked a transition for WIPO from the mandate it inherited in 1967 from BIRPI, to promote the protection of intellectual property, to one that involved the more complex task of promoting technology transfer and economic development.

Unlike other branches of the United Nations, WIPO has significant financial resources independent of the contributions from its Member States. In 2006, over 90% of its income of just over CHF 250 million was expected to be generated from the collection of fees by the *International Bureau* (IB) under the intellectual property application and registration systems which it administers (the Patent Co-operation Treaty, the Madrid system for trade marks and the Hague system for industrial designs).

In October 2004, WIPO agreed to adopt a proposal offered by Argentina and Brazil, the "Proposal for the Establishment of a

Development Agenda for WIPO"-from the Geneva Declaration on the Future of the World Intellectual Property Organization. This proposal was well-supported by developing countries. The agreed "WIPO Development Agenda" (composed of over 45 recommendations) was the culmination of a long process of transformation for the organization from one that had historically been primarily aimed at protecting the interests of right holders, to one that has increasingly incorporated the interests of other stakeholders in the international intellectual property system as well as integrating into the broader corpus of international law on human rights, environment and economic co-operation.

A number of civil society bodies have been working on a draft Access to Knowledge (A2K) treaty which they would like to see introduced.

In December 2011, WIPO published its first World Intellectual Property Report on the Changing Face of Innovation, the first such report of the new Office of the Chief Economist.[12] WIPO is also a co-publisher of the Global Innovation Index.

In April 2012, Fox News first reported the shipment of computers by WIPO to North Korea and Iran, in an alleged violation of U.S. and U.N. sanctions, triggering an investigation by the U.S. State Department. WIPO reacted by stating that the shipment did not violate the U.N. sanctions against North Korea, and that this was "part of WIPO's standard technical assistance program to developing countries", later announcing in July 2012 that it would discontinue the provision of computers to all countries. After a preliminary assessment, the U.S. State Department announced on July 24, 2012 that WIPO didn't appear to have violated U.N. sanctions. In September 2012, an independent investigative report, commissioned by WIPO found that while the shipments were legal, they were "unjustified" and states that WIPO violated American export control legislation. The report also said that the violations were worse than was previously known. In November 2012, a US Congressional investigation team arrives in Geneva to facilitate questioning members of the WIPO staff.

Information network

WIPO has established WIPOnet, a global information network. The project seeks to link over 300 intellectual property offices (IP offices) in all WIPO Member States. In addition to providing a means of secure communication among all connected parties, WIPO net is the foundation for WIPO's intellectual property services.

Director-General(s)

- 1st - Georg Bodenhausen - 1970-1973
- 2nd - Árpád Bogsch - 1973-1997
- 3rd - Kamil Idris - 1997-2008
- 4th - Francis Gurry - 2008-till date.

Chapter 10

Demand Forecasts – Concept and Methods

Demand forecasting

Demand forecasting is the activity of estimating the quantity of a product or service that consumers will purchase. Demand forecasting involves techniques including both informal methods, such as educated guesses, and quantitative methods, such as the use of historical sales data or current data from test markets. Demand forecasting may be used in making pricing decisions, in assessing future capacity requirements, or in making decisions on whether to enter a new market.

All business firms must forecast the demand for their products or services to plan to survive and grow. The economics literature provides them a list of demand forecasting techniques to help the manager to plan. Demand forecasting assumes greater importance, in view of the changes coupled with information revolution happening almost in all countries, to enable optimal utilization of the available resources in ultimately transforming the economy smoothly. Thus, it becomes crucial to evaluate the validity of the popular demand forecasting techniques.

Economists, through their varied definitions, generally mean demand (of whatever type) to be the need for the commodity or service (let us call this as a 'product' plus the willingness to buy plus the capacity to buy or the purchasing power or their money income. That is when we refer to the concept 'demand' we are, in fact, referring to a group of three variables, namely (i) the need, (ii) the willingness and (iii) the money income. Now let us see what is 'forecasting' a variable? Now Forecasting simply refers to assigning a value to a variable at a future point of time (whether short-term, medium-term or long-term) for instance, the value of x at point of time t+n. i.e. xt+n. Therefore, demand forecasting refers to measuring and assigning a value represented by a number to the quantity of product 'x' that will be demanded at a future point of time.

The Demand Forecasting Techniques

The economic literature gives a number of techniques for forecasting demand broadly classified as objective methods using statistical or mathematical approach and subjective methods using intuition based on experience, intelligence and judgement.

I. Some of the popular objective methods used are :

1. Extrapolation methods,
2. Regression models,
3. Leading indicator methods,
4. Econometric methods,
5. End-user or input-output models, etc.

II. Some of the popular subjective methods are :

1. Consumer surveys,
2. Expert opinion surveys and
3. Test market methods, etc.

Objective Methods of Demand-forecasting

1. Extrapolation methods

The **extrapolation methods** in general logically extend the behaviour of the variable, from time series data, into the future :

i) The **trend-fitting** methods observes the direction (increase, decrease or the trend, cycles, seasonality, randomness) of the movement or behaviour of the demand and assume that the behavior will be exhibited in future also. This is done methodically (least-squares method) by 'assuming' time as the cause of demand. Ultimately the trend-fitting method gives the value of demand as a 'refined average' of the past values.

ii) The family of the **smoothing methods** (simple smoothing method, exponential smoothing method, moving average method, autoregressive moving average method, auto-regressive interactive moving average method) forecast or measure the demand based on 'averaging' the past values of x and 'refining' the averages in various degrees and stages) so that the deviation of the actual values of the past from its mean is minimum. The basis of this method is logically to extend the average value into the future point of time. Ultimately these methods say that "on an average" the demand for x is "an average of x".

2. The regression method

The **regression method** determines the degree of influence (coefficients) of cause or causes (determinants) of demand for x, significance and reliability from the past values of the 'assumed' causes or causes advised by the economic theories using a statistical method based on the least squares of the deviation of the observed value from its mean (i.e. the least-squares method). The degree of influence of these causes is in the form of an equation and it calculates the value of the demand variable. The essence of this method is measuring the future value of demand based on its causes, assuming the absence of problems, such as autocorrelation, multicollinearity and the like errors.

3. The Leading indicator or Barometric methods

(leading-indicator, lagging -indicator or coincidental-indicator) use another variable other than the variable 'x' that is being forecast. But those variables are 'indicative' of the behaviour or direction of the movement of the demand for x.

These indicator variables may be or may not be the 'causes' of demand. The essence of this method is that the behaviour of demand for 'x' is not directly observed from the variable that is being forecast. Instead the behaviour of demand for 'x' is observed indirectly through another variable (proxy variable!) which is indicative of the behaviour of demand for 'x'. There are three types of indicator variables :

i) The **Leading indicators** are those variables which always lead the demand for 'x', i.e. these variables precede the demand variable in occurrence along the time scale.

ii) The **Lagging indicators** are those variables that always lag behind the demand variable, i.e. the demand variable precedes these variables in occurrence along the time scale.

iii) **The Coincidental indicators** are those variables that occur along with the demand variable at the same time along the time scale. The essence of this method is that it "assumes" that by studying the behaviour of an indicator variable (cause variable or non-cause variable), it studies the behaviour of the demand for 'x'. Therefore it logically follows that forecasting the future value of the indicator variable is equivalent to forecasting the demand variable under study.

4. The Econometric methods

The **Econometric methods** of demand forecasting is estimating the demand equation based on the degree of influence of the causes (determinants) on demand for 'x' which, in turn, is measured by the degree of influence of the causes of the determinants of demand for 'x'. The relationships across the demand, demand determinants and their determinants are established as an equation estimated from their past behaviour using the least-squares method.

5. The End-User method

The **End-User method** is also used to forecast demand based on the end-use to which the products are put to. Based on the quantum of end-use the demand for the product is extrapolated.

B Subjective Methods of Demand Forecasting

Basically the subjective methods are designed to know the 'intentions' or 'presence or absence of the willingness' of the buyers given the determinants of demand like the price of the product, quality, quantity, etc. through intelligent questions, interviews or questionnaires (direct or mailed).

1. Complete enumeration or census method

Complete enumeration or census method questions (either face to face or through a mailed questionnaire) all the consumers, without excluding any one, to know their 'intentions' of buying. **Sample survey method** questions, to know the intentions, only a selected representative sample of the whole population of consumers and logically extends the inferred findings to the whole population. These methods simply sum up what the consumers say or opine and 'assume' that what they say is true and correct and that they will do the same! The basis of this method is that demand is based purely on consumers' opinion about the quantity, quality, etc. and that demand is not based on the demand-determinants or it's end-use.

2. Expert opinion survey method

Expert opinion survey method bases its subjective forecast on the 'opinion' of the experts instead of the consumers. That is the demand of a product is set equal to the 'quantity' pronounced by these experts! If the forecast quantity is reasoned through an interactive procedure justified by the experts, then this method is called as the **reasoned expert survey or Delphi Technique**. If the forecast is not reasoned out, then it is known as the **simple expert opinion poll**.

3. The test-market method

The **test-market method** is based on learning or knowing the demand for a product by actually selling or experimenting with the sales of the product. A product is simply introduced into a test-market and its demand is observed and logically extending the behaviour of demand to markets similar to the test-market. The essence of these demand-forecasting techniques is presented in Table 1. Economists say that there are no one single best technique for forecasting demand and that all these techniques have their own limitations.

❑❑❑

Chapter 11

Valuation of Timber and Non-timber Products

Timber Valuation

Starting with a complete timber cruise (timber inventory) and ending with a comprehensive report, our approach to timber appraisals emphasizes objectively collected data to determine not only timber volumes, but also unit prices to provide clients appraisal-level confidence in the value of their timber.

Why do people need their timber valued?

When a property is purchased, the purchase price is allocated between timber and land. The timber values are used for timber tax purposes, both when timber income is realized and when the property is eventually sold. A timber valuation is a necessity when valuing a large forested property (forestland appraisal), as timber is usually the major price driver of the total value. Timber values are absolutely necessary, when buying or selling a forested property for the same reason. Prior to a timber harvest, a timber valuation is especially critical, if the timber is to be sold for a single fixed price.

How is timber valued?

Determining the value of timber requires not only the careful and scientifically conducted measurement of trees, but also the thorough analysis of timber markets and how value will be recognized in the measured timber. At **fountains**, we apply equal care to both aspects of timber valuation. The objective is not merely to put a value to a measured volume of timber, but to truly appraise the market value of the timber, as it stands on the land.

The value of timber as it stands uncut is referred to as stumpage and is essentially the price paid at the mill, less the cost of logging and transportation; this figure is then applied to the volume of standing timber.

Volumes on a tract of land vary according to the history of land use as well as a variety of biological factors. Prices vary according to market demand and production costs.

Mill prices tend to be competitive with each other and driven by the market and the price of lumber. Mills buy timber according to species and grade. Grades are based on the quality and size of individual stems. Most mill price levels are based on the availability of timber and the market for the final product.

Logging costs tend to be more variable and are related to the specific property situation, and include felling the timber, removing it from the woods, and delivering it to the mill. Logging costs can vary tremendously according to the type of equipment used, the distance from the mill, the size and distribution of the timber to be cut, the topographic features of the land, and the condition of both internal and external access.

Species	Volume MBF/CD	Unit Price Range Low	High	Likely	Total Value Likely
Sawtimber - MBF (International 1/4")					
Red Oak	2,494	430.00	550.00	480.00	1,197,100
White Pine	1,253	130.00	170.00	150.00	188,000
Yellow /Black Birch	222	190.00	300.00	240.00	53,300
Red Oak Veneer	38	600.00	1,100.00	900.00	34,200
Hemlock	491	20.00	50.00	40.00	19,600
Red Maple	127	60.00	180.00	130.00	16,500
White Oak	101	100.00	200.00	130.00	13,100
Red Oak Small Diam.	126	35.00	120.00	100.00	12,600
Red Pine	117	60.00	100.00	75.00	8,800
Red Oak Pallet	71	35.00	120.00	100.00	7,100
Pallet / Grade 3	200	15.00	50.00	35.00	7,000
White Pine Pallet	81	35.00	100.00	40.00	3,200
Paper Birch	22	80.00	160.00	120.00	2,600
White Ash	9	100.00	220.00	120.00	1,100
Basswood	8	25.00	60.00	45.00	400
Beech	3	20.00	50.00	40.00	100
Pulpwood - Cords					
Hardwoods	14,510	5.00	14.00	8.00	116,100
Hemlock	560	8.00	18.00	12.00	6,700
White Pine	1,540	1.00	5.00	3.00	4,600

Totals				
Sawtimber Total	5,363	MBF		$1,564,700
Sawtimber Per Acre	3.350	MBF		$977
Sawtimber Per Comm. Acre	3.510	MBF		$1,024
Cordwood Total	16,610	Cords		$127,400
Cordwood Per Acre	10.4	Cords		$80
Cordwood Per Comm. Acre	10.9	Cords		$83
			Total Per Acre	$1,057

	Low	High	Likely
Total Value	$1,561,000	$1,867,000	$1,692,000

Economic Valuation of Non-Timber Forest Products (NTFPs)

Introduction

The term "Forest product" almost immediately brings to mind wood and wood-based products, but there are equally important non-wood products that are procured from the forest. These include all botanical and other natural products extracted from the forest other than timber. Non-timber forest products (NTFPs) are components of the forest system that exist in nature and are generally not cultivated. They are non-timber, but can be made of wood.

What are NTFPs?

Non-timber forest products (NTFPs) are plants or plant parts that have perceived economic or consumption value sufficient to encourage their collection and removal from the forest. That is, they are those items harvested or removed from the forest lands for private use or for re-sale (excluding, saw-timber, pole timber, natural gas, oil, sand, gravel, shale and building stone all of which are covered under other sections). It can also be referred to as all the resources/products that may be extracted from forest ecosystem and are utilised within the household or are marketed or have social, cultural or religious significance (FAO, 1990). These include plants and plant materials used for food, fuel, storage and fodder, medicine, cottage and wrapping materials, biochemical, as well as animals, birds, reptiles and fishes, for food and feather.

NTFPs which are harvested from within and on the edges of natural and disturbed forest, may be all or part of living or dead plants, lichens, fungi, or other forest organisms. It, therefore, represents a diversity of potential products sought after by a wide variety of people on a continuum of scales and intensities. Unlike timber-based products, NTFPs came from a large variety of plant parts and are formed into a diverse set of products: leaves & twigs that may be component of decorative arrangements, food items, such as fruits, fungi and juices, wood carved or woven into pieces of art or utilitarian objects and roots, leaves and bark processed into herbal remedies or medicines. Like timber, NTFPs may further be processed into consumer oriented products. Description of these products may pose a problem due to lack of information concerning the distribution systems used to get the products to final consumers. NTFPs are found in a wide variety of outlets e.g. health food store, pharmacy, etc. unlike timber-based products. People have benefitted from those plants for many generations. In some cases, NTFPs according to chamberlain (1998) contribute significantly to local and regional economics; and with the current trend in the trade and use of NTFPs, it is bound to grow substantially over the next decades.

Classification of NTFPs

The number of products available from NTFP is considered to be staggering. Energy (1998) identified 138 products from 80 forest species in Michigan Upper Peninsula. The United Nations and Food & Agricultural Organisation claimed that at least 150 non-wood products are found in international markets.

Classifying these products into like categories is an important first step of understanding the NTFPs industry. NTFPs can be broadly classified into edibles and non-edibles. The former include edible plants & animals, honey, oils, fish, spices, etc. while non-edible products include grasses, ornamental plants, oil for cosmetic use, medicinal products, etc.

These two classes can further be divided into four general categories:

1. **Edibles :** Edibles, such as mushroom, the most well known and documented edible forest products and many other food products gathered from the forest. Since most of these products are not traded widely and are usually collected and consumed by the harvesters themselves, it is difficult to assess their economic magnitudes. These products include ferns, berries or other fruits, nuts, ramps (wild onions), herbs and spices.

2. **Medicinal and dietary supplements:** This includes plant based products that are processed into medicines. Beginning in the late eighteenth century, over 100 plant species indigenous to the U.S were commonly accepted for their medicinal properties. The majority are wild harvested and traded as botanical products (Foster, 1995).

3. **Floral products :** It includes pine boughs, grapevines, ferns, and other plant products used for decorative applications. These unique forest products may appear in floral arrangements, dried flower decorations, and ornaments, common example include

products made from pine boughs, grapevines, moss, ferns, flowers, cone, mistle toe and holly (Hammett *et al.,* 1998).

4. **Specialty wood products :** These include handicrafts, carving and turnings, musical instrument containers (basket), special furniture pieces as well as utensils. In general, speciality wood products are considered non traditional, if they are produced directly from trees and not from lumber or timber purchased from mills. In other words, the tree may not need to be cut down to produce these items.

Historical Perspective

The gathering of NTFP is as old as the human species itself. Wild food and other items from the forest provided food, shelter, medicine and materials for ceremonies and worship. When people began to domesticate plants and animals, they became less dependent on wild food and other forest material.

Native Americans traditionally used plants and plant products for food, and medicine, and shared this knowledge with early settlers. They used the bark of trees for housing, branches and stems for utensils and other useful items. This traditional forest product became an integral part of rural economies and many techniques are still in use today. According to Hammett *et al* (1998), there was a dramatic increase in demand for natural products in the 90'sincluding those of NTFPs. This is traceable to a number of factors which includes a growing interest in alternative medicines and homeopathy.

Homeopathy, according to Encarta (2006) is an alternative system of medicine developed in the early 19th century, based on the concept that a disease can be cured, when a patient is treated with minute quantities of a substance that produces symptoms of the disease in a healthy person. Homeopathy focuses on healing the underlying cause of disease, not simply eliminating the symptoms caused by the disease.

Economic Value and Growth of NTFPs

From the economic viewpoint, NTFPs are equally important as wood based products. About 150 types of NTFPs are significant in international trade. They are also increasingly being acknowledged for their role in sustainable development and conservation of ecosystem. Upto 80 per cent of the population in developing countries depends on NTFPs for subsistence, both economically and for nutrition.

NTFPs are especially important to women in developing countries from Latin America to Asia and Africa (Gbadebo *et al.*, 1999).

In the past, the rationale for forest conservation was simply to sustain the forest productive role for the timber industry. This has, however, changed in many countries over the past 15 years, another view that acknowledges the importance of local use of forest has emerged. With the rise of extractive reserves in Brazil, Community Forestry in Nepal, Joint Forest Management in India and similar initiatives in many other countries, local people are gaining access to significant benefits from NTFPs. NTFPs are often common property resources, like fuel wood, fodder, charcoal, poles, medicinal plants and a variety of food stuffs, such as fruits and nuts, mushrooms, fibre and resins (Arnold, 1995).

Markets for NTFPs to add value at the local level are not well known, but are thought to have significant impact on rural economies. A few of the edible forest products are prominent enough to generate national economic data. According to Foster (1995), the U.S exported about 77tons of wild harvested American ginseng valued at more than $21m in 1993. Two years earlier, Virginia exported about 6.5tons of ginseng worth over $1.8m (0' Rourke, 1993).

The NTFPs sector is rapidly growing, perhaps faster than the timber industry and it is expected to grow more in the future. According to Mater, (New York Times, 1996), the market for forest products other than trees has mushroomed by nearly 20% annually over the past years. It was also noted that the U.S herbal medicine market grew at an estimated annual rate of 13-15% with sales of medicinal herbs, a forecast that US economy would earn $5billion in the year 2000. New York Times (1996) reported that in the Pacific North-west, mosses, ferms and other plants have sustained the commercial floral products industry and contributed more than $ 125 million to the region's economy.

Importance of NTFPs to Livelihood Security

NTFPs are a dependable source of income and food supply in the rural areas. However, it is a diminishing resource as a result of its dependency on land which is known to be under pressure of depletion from agriculture and development of public infrastructures. Non-timber forest products constitute a critical component of food security and it is an important source of income for the poor in many developing countries. Several opportunities for improved rural development are linked to NTFP. In many areas, rural populations are traditionally depended on local forest resources to provide additional income through collection and marketing of NTFPs. Where employment opportunities from traditional industries are declining, workers looking for alternative income sources often turn to collection of these products from nearby forest.

Millions of people throughout the world make extensive use of biological products from the wild i.e. NTFPs. They are harvested for both subsistence and commercial use either regularly or as a fall back during times of need. They add to people's livelihood security, especially for rural dwellers. NTFPs may also have cultural significance and value (Cooks *et al.*, 2003).

Charlie *et al.* (2004) looked into the role and importance of NTFPs in daily lives of rural people in South Africa and discovered that more than 85% household used products, such as wild spinaches, fuel wood, wooden utensils, edible fruits, etc. Also, they reported that more than half of the household investigated made use of edible insects, wood for construction Bushmeat, wild honey and reeds for weaving.

In Nigeria, food security of rural dwellers is improved by growing trees in the home gardens and on farms. Leaves, rattan, honey, sap, gums from the small scale industries are important sources of income (Okafor *et al.*, 1994).

Due to the diverse varieties for species obtainable from NTFPs a lot of household were able to meet their immediate needs by collecting these products from the nearby forest. While other households earn income to meet other needs through the marketing of NTFPs harvested.

Against this background, NTFPs are obviously very important as they contribute to meeting food and other basic needs. They provide a source of input into the agricultural system, help households control exposure to risk of various kinds. A better understanding of the magnitude and nature of the role of NTFPs is, therefore, central to making decision about forest management that adequately reflects society's demand upon the forest resource.

Constraints Facing the NTFPs Sector

NTFPs when compared with timber products have historically been neglected by governments. The capacity to promote sustainable use of NTFP and facilitate increased financial benefits to local users, as incentives for forest conservation is consequently low. There are yet gaps in understanding the range of products used from forests, their taxonomic classification, socio-economic values, technical packages and the policy contexts for their sustainable use.

Also, the existing expertise and knowledge is not well-documented or is inaccessible. This means that many are duplicated while many important issues remain neglected. There is equally a lack of appropriate methods and tools to promote sustainable use of NTFPs and successfully regulate trade and the form policy development i.e. policy development is still largely disconnected from field experiences.

The challenge for coming years is to develop proper tools and methods for sustainable extraction of NTFP and regulation of its trade. This can be achieved by efficiently using the existing knowledge and experience of facilitators, entrepreneurs and researchers in the region. This involves steps, such as identifying, connecting and engaging such people in a range of networking activities that stimulate the flow of information and learning, and that yield products of immediate interest and utility to the concerned NTFP conservation initiative.

Considering the issue of sustainable production of NTFPs, there are a number of challenges to be met, some of which includes the disappearing of forest cover, inequitable market access of marginalized population and monopolization of high value NTFP by logging and poaching mafia.

Valuing Non-timber Forest Product

Value is not the inherent property of an entity. It is only a measure of a relationship between a subject and the object of valuation within a context (time and place or hypothetical scenario). There is a fundamental distinction to be made between a valuation exercise that sets out to explain how choices are made by individual resource users and one that seeks to maximize community or societal well-being.

A societal perspective requires a broader approach, usually some type of social cost-benefit analysis and is necessarily a normative exercise because it involves judgement about what outcomes are socially preferable (Costanza *et al.,* 1997).

Appropriate method of valuation depends on the objective of the study. Two journal articles were reviewed for the purpose of this study.

Murphy *et al* (2005) undertook a survey to evaluate the flow of Non-Timber Forest Products in a district in India, where NTFPs were collected in four different forest zone of the district. The study aimed at preparing an inventory of the NTFPs extracted in the region, estimate the quantity of NTFP gathered by locals and the forest department and finally estimate the financial income derived from NTFPs extracted. The households were classified into three i.e. large farmers garden owners and landless labourers based on the farm holdings. In each class, if the number of the household was less than 5, 100% sampling was done; otherwise 25% of the household were randomly selected for the survey.

The result indicated that all classes of NTFPs were available in the district forest zones and they were qualified based on the kind of species extracted e.g. fuel wood measured in kilogram/year i.e. weight of fuel wood fetched on an annual basis. Fodder, honey mushrooms, wild mangoes, etc. collected was measured in kg/household/year.

The financial valuation of NTFPs which indicate the income of the farming household was carried out irrespective of the gathering household. That is, the total population of each forest zone was considered wholly. The financial valuation of the quantities of NTFPs gathered was estimated by using the current market value and measured in kg/ha/yr. There were variations in the estimated value realized per household as well as differences in their financial value across the zones considered. It was also reported that a comparison of the annual value of timber with a ten year mean (1985-94) of Rs.239 million and NTFPs value of Rs 685 million for the year (1995-96) indicates that NTFPs contribute doubly to the economy and benefits flow directly to local communities.

The authors were able to value NTFPs by directly using the current market price to estimate the income of the communities with the quantities of NTFPs gathered. However, financial valuation using market prices could not account for the elements of cost involved in the production and distribution of NTFPs e.g. cost of labour and transportation. Economic analysis would have given a clearer picture of the real value.

Also, the author did not justify why he chose to sample 100% when household was less than 5 and 25% otherwise in each class. An inconsistency in the unit of measurement was observed, while some NTFPs were measured in kg/households/year, some were measured in Kg/year without an indication of the value of land cultivated. But the financial valuation considered the land value used.

The households were classified unto large farmers, garden owners and landless labourers based on their farm holdings, this classification is not exhaustive, it should include other classification like small farmers, and possibly medium farmers among others. In addition, the author did not indicate what was responsible for the observed variations in the estimated value of NTFPs realized by the households as well as the differences in the financial value per hectare of NTFPs across the four zones considered.

A similar study by Shacleton *et al.* (2004) on the importance of NTFPs in rural livelihood security focused on the extent of use and value of NTFPs at a broad scale.

They value their NTFPs collected in two ways :

1. By using 'direct use value' which was based on the farm gate prices and input cost was considered. This method of valuation acknowledges cost-benefit analysis.
2. Also, NTFPs were valued based on their contribution to livelihood i.e. by assisting household to cope in times of adversity manifested at sudden changes in the economic and social or biophysical environment e.g. flood, death of head of household, etc. Here the "direct use value" of NTFPs used during period of adversity does not adequately reflect their true value because it does not account for emergency insurance component of use during the times of hardship.

In these situations, the changed or increased use of NTFPs is typically a coping strategy, with the products providing a safety net for the household.

In the articles reviewed, there was an assumption that underestimates possible post harvest losses and the market cost of perishable NTFPs. The authors also assumed that all the NTFPs are tradable, this may not be true. For non-traded NTFPs, non-market prices are supposed to be used. The study will be richer, if the authors had separated the NTFPs between Traded and non-traded before estimating their financial value. Also, no indication was made about the estimate of the value of NTFPs used for domestic purpose by households.

Economic Valuation of Non-Timber Forest Product

Value is the worth of a product or service to an individual or a like-minded group in a given context, often involving a complex of relationships (Brown, 1984). Values are of concern not just in the field of economics, for example, they are dealt with by philosophers in their treatment of ethics. Economic values are human oriented and human assigned. Values are specific to a given context and situation.

Forest valuation should, therefore, always be situation specific and result should be attributed back only to the group studied and to the actual context and situation studied. (FAO, 1995).

Types of forest values

Economic value associated with forest can be classified into four categories :

i) Direct-use values (including consumptive & non-consumptive values).

ii) Indirect-use values.

iii) Option values

iv) Existence and bequest (inheritance/donation) values

An addition of all these value is the total economic value. The purpose of valuation is to make the value of each forest use explicit and not necessarily to put a total value on nature (Michael, 1995).

Total Economic Value (TEV) is an aggregate of:

1. **Total use value**: This can be divided into direct-use value, indirect-use value and option value.
2. **Total non-value**: include Existence & bequest value.

Classification of Forest Values

1. Direct use value are associated with

- Consumptive uses:
  - a) Commercial & industrial market goods, Fuel wood, timber, pulpwood poles, fruits, animals, medicines, etc.
  - b) Domestic non-market goods and services (fuel wood, non-commercial non-wood products, animals, fruits, etc.).

- Non consumption uses:

  a) Recreation (jungle, cruises wildlife, photography, trekking)

  b) Science and Education (forest studies)

2. Indirect use values are associated with :

- Environmental protection
- Waster shed protection, nutrient recycling, soil fertility agricultural productivity.
- Gas exchange, contribution to climate stabilization.
- Habitat and protection of biodiversity.
- Aesthetic, cultural and spiritual values.

3. Option value

- People may value the option to use a forest in the future. Although such values are difficult to measure in economic term, they should be recognized in valuing the contribution of forest to human welfare.

4. Existence & Bequest values

- People may value forests purely for its existence without the intension of using it directly in the future.
- People may value forest as a bequest to their children. It is not so easy to compute these value separately, as they are dependent on each other e.g. the felling of trees by harvesting may degrade (or improve) the habitat for specific birds and animals.

Measures of Value

Three main types of measure can be used for forest valuation :

a) Direct market price (as used by Murphy *et al* 2005),

b) Indirect market price (as used by shackleton *et al* 2004) and

c) Non-market estimates of values

The first two measures are based on estimate of exchange values, where buyers and sellers exchange goods or service for money or other goods and services. In the case of indirect market price, we have assumptions regarding proxy market conditions and low buyers and sellers will behave under different circumstances (Dixon *et al.*, 1994). However, non-market values estimate the willingness of buyers to purchaser or pay for specific goods or services under defined conditions. Non-market value estimates are not directly comparable with market based exchange values.

Summary and Conclusion

The simplest and most commonly used method of valuing any good or service is to take its market price. Thus, the price of NTFPs directly harvested from the forest determines their value. When these products and services are not directly traded in the market, their value can be derived from their contribution in other production processes or their impact on the prices of other commodities. NTFPs values can also be determined through assessing the cost of man-made products, infrastructure or technologies that could replace these goods. It could also be valued by what people are willing to pay for the goods and services, or their willingness to accept compensation for their loss.

❑❑❑

Chapter 12

Marketable Surplus and Marketed Surplus

Marketable Surplus

The marketable surplus is that quantity of the produce which can be made available to the non-farm population of the country. It is the residual left with the farmers after meeting his family consumption, farm requirements, social and religions payments. There is inverse relationship between price and marketable surplus.

MS = P – C Where, Ms – Marketable surplus,

P–Total Production

C –Total family requirement

Total production = Area x production per unit

Total requirement = Family req. + livestock req. + seed material req. + other req., etc.

Factors Affecting Marketable Surplus

The marketable surplus differs from region to region and within the same region, from crop to crop. It also varies from farm to farm. On a particular farm, the quantity of marketable surplus depends on the following factors :

1. **Size of holding :** There is positive relationship between the size of the holding and the marketable surplus.
2. **Production of Commodity :** The higher the production on a farm, the larger will be the marketable surplus, and vice versa.
3. **Price of the Commodity :** The price of the commodity and the marketable surplus have a positive as well as negative relationship, depending upon whether one considers the short and long run or the micro and macro levels.

4. **Size of family :** The larger the number of members in a family, the smaller the surplus on the farm.
5. **Requirements of seeds and feed :** The higher the requirement for these uses, the smaller the marketable surplus of the crop.
6. **Nature of commodity :** The marketable surplus of non food crops is generally higher than that for food crops, e.g. In the case of cotton, jute and rubber, the quantity retained for family consumption is either negligible or very small part of the total output. But for these crops, a very large proportion of total output is marketable surplus. Even among food crops commodities like sugarcane, spices and oilseeds which require some processing before final consumption, the marketable surplus as a proportion of total output is larger than that for other food crops.
7. **Consumption Habits :** The quantity of output retained by the farm family depends on the consumption habits. For example, in Punjab, rice forms a relatively small proportion of total cereals consumed by farm families compared to those in southern and eastern states. Therefore, out of a given output of paddy/rice, Punjab farmers sell a greater proportion than that sold by rice eating farmers of other states.

Marketed Surplus

Marketed Surplus is the quantity of the produce which the producer, farmer or collector actually sale in the market irrespective of his requirement for family consumption. The marketed surplus may be more or less or equal to marketable surplus.

Case 1. The marketed surplus is more than the marketable surplus when the farmer retains a smaller quantity of crop than his actual family and farm requirements. This is true, especially of small and marginal farmers whose need for cash is immediate. The situation of selling more than marketable surplus is termed as distress or forced sale. Such farmers generally buy the produce from the market in a later period to meet their requirements.

Case 2. The marketed surplus is less than the marketable surplus, when the farmer retains some of the surplus produce. This situation holds good under the following situations :

a) Large farmers generally sell less than the marketable surplus because of their better retention capacity. They retain extra produce in the hope that they would get a higher price in the later period. Sometimes farmers retain the produce even up to the next production season.

b) Farmer may substitute one crop for another crop either for family consumption purpose or other farm requirements because of the variation in prices. With the fall in the price of the crop relative to a competing crop, farmer may consume more of the first and less of the second crop.

Case 3. The marketed surplus may be equal to the marketable surplus when the farmer neither retains more nor less than his requirement. This holds true for perishable commodities and agricultural raw materials (like cotton, jute, etc.) for the average farmer.

Estimation of marketed and marketable surplus at the level of individual farmer is easy. There have been a larger number of studies which provides the estimates of marketed and marketable surplus at micro level. Apart from the use of such estimates for ascertaining the marketed surplus at the national level, such micro studies have been used to bring out the nature and extent of distress sale of food grains by small and marginal farmers.

Problem 1 : Consider the following data of a case of a farm of Mr. Jagdish for the year 2015-16 (July to June).

There are six adult units in the family of Mr. Jagdish. He also maintains two milch animals. Mr. Jagdish sold 120 quintals of wheat, 15 quintals of barley, 48 quintals of mustard, 40 quintals of gram, 60 quintals of bajra and 30 quintals of paddy at different times between July 2013 and June 2014. So, with the help of this information, the marketable and marketed surplus of different crop of this farmer can be worked out.

Table 1. The total production and the requirements of the farm and families are as follows:

Crop	Area in ha	Production (q/ha)	Seed requirement	Consumption requirement (per unit)	Requirement for per livestock unit
1. Wheat	8	20	6.0	2.00	2.00 for artisans
2. Barley	2	12	1.0	0.50	-
3. Mustard	5	10	0.4	0.10	-
4. Gram	5	10	2.5	0.25	1.00 for artisans
5. Bajra	15	6	3.0	1.00	-
6. Paddy	5	8	2.0	-	2.50 per milch cow

Table 2. Calculate the total production and the requirements of the farm and families.

Crop	Total Production (Area X Productivity)	Seed requirement	Consumption requirement (No.of units X requirement per unit)	Other requirements	Total requirements
1. Wheat					
2. Barley					
3. Mustard					
4. Gram					
5. Bajra					
6. Paddy					

Table 3. Calculate the marketable and marketed surplus of different products for this farm.

Crops	Total Production (q)	Total requirements (q)	Marketable surplus (q)	Marketed surplus (q)	As percentage of production	
					Marketable surplus (q)	Marketed surplus (q)
1. Wheat						
2. Barley						
3. Mustard						
4. Gram						
5. Bajra						
6. Paddy						

Inference:

Problem 2: Calculate marketable surplus, marketed surplus and percentage of production for marketable surplus and marketed surplus from the following information.

There are 8 members in the family of Mr. Sahuram. Mr. Sahuram sold 193 quintal of Soap nut, 31 quintals of Nutmeg, 71 quintals of Amla, 72 quintals of Safed Masli, 111 quintals of Shatawari and 42 quintals of Garcinia fruits in Sirsi market in April-2012. The household consumption per head annually for soapnut is 120 kg and Shatawari is 65 kg.

Crop	Area (ha)	Productivity (Q/ha)	Seed Requirement
1. Soapnut	12.0	25	6.20
2. Nutmeg	2.9	15	1.90
3. Amla	8.0	13	0.90
4. Safed Masli	8.0	14	3.41
5. Shatawari	20.0	8	3.02
6.Garcinia fruits	9.0	11	2.97

Inference:

❑❑❑

Chapter 13

Systems and Methods of Sale of Forest Produce

Systems of Sale of Forest Produce

1. Lump Sum Sale

- All systems of sales under which a fixed sum is paid for produce; whether the exact quantity of such produce is known or not.
- The sales may be by auction, tender or direct.
- Sale price is usually realized in installments.

2. Payment on Outturn

- Includes the sales when the amount fixed corresponds with the actual amount of produce sold or extracted.
- Royalty may be on volume, weight, quantity and may not include a guarantee of the outturns be extracted.
- Methods of working are closely linked with systems of sale and common methods of working and sale are:

  1. Sale of whole coupe or area
  2. Sale of standing trees
  3. Sale of a few selected trees
  4. Sale by means of license or permit
  5. Sale by communication system
  6. Extraction without previous permit or agreement.

Methods of Sale

The common methods of selling forest produce are as under:

1. Sale by private bargain
2. Sale to the highest bidder
   a) by public auction
   b) by tender
      i) Sealed tender,
      ii) Open tender
3. Sale by royalty or fixed tariff.

1. Sale by Private Bargain

When an owner deals with a single purchaser and negotiates the price after mutual discussion, the result is the sale by private bargain; In such deals the parties are guided by results of past sales and current market trends. This method is applicable under the following circumstances:

- For ordinary transactions, where the quantity to be sold is small
- Produce for which demand is limited, where one person or a firm desires to purchase some produce for which there is no general demand, and no keen competition is expected, as for example, when a few selected trees or logs are required for some particular industry. The price may be fixed according to current market rates or past sales.
- To popularize the use of a particular species for a new industry. In such cases even a low price may be charged in the beginning to give an impetus (encourage) to the industry and to create keen competition in due course.

The method has the following advantages:

- Fair price can be obtained for produce, which is not much in demand.
- Future markets can be created by giving scope to a new industry
- Auction rings can be broken.

- When market is dull or overstocked, this method gives better results than open auction
- Saves auction expenses.

2. Sale to Highest Bidder

The characteristic of this method is that the price is fixed by the purchaser and the produce is divided among the purchasers according to their own requirement.

a) Sale by Public Auction (Auction – Public sale by bidding)

This is the public sale by increasing the price by the intending purchasers, outbidding each other. The highest bidder becomes the purchaser. To prevent unreasonable low price being offered, a minimum price is fixed, known as the 'Upset price' or 'Reserve price.' It is suitable where free keen competition exists but is unsuitable for slack times, when market is over stacked and competition poor.

It is a fair method of sale and if competition is keen and no rings are formed amongst purchasers, therefore, good prices are obtained. A variety of ordinary auction is the 'Dutch auction' but is not an auction in the true sense. In this auction, the auctioneer commences with a prohibitively high price, and then progressively calling out at regular intervals, reduces by a fixed sum, until one of the purchasers signifies his acceptance of the last price figure proclaimed.

b) Sale by Tender

Under this system intending purchasers make offers on or before a fixed date stating the price, they are willing to pay. Such tenders are of two kinds-sealed and open.

Sealed Tenders

The date, time and place of opening tenders is notified in advance. The tenderers or their authorized agents can be present. Each tender is accompanied by Earnest Money Deposit in the form of a treasury *challan*, Demand draft, which is pledged to the competent authority. This method is quite popular and fair though not the best method in getting maximum returns.

Open Tenders

The intending purchasers send their offers before a fixed date; their offers being known to all who may like to participate. It is a sort of **tender-cum-auction** management that may or may not be combined with bargain. Sale by tender is suitable for the type of produce, which has fairly constant value. When the market is slack and overstocked, it is preferable to have open auction.

3. Sale by Royalty or Fixed Tariff

The feature of this method is that the price is fixed by the seller who also provides for the distribution of the produce among its consumers. Royalty may be based on weight number, quantity or volume, or it may be 'advalorem' royalty which is in terms of a certain percentage on its market value. The schedule of rates is based on average sale price obtained in auctions or tenders, market price, or rates fixed in adjoining areas and cost of production.

The royalty schedule is therefore revised from time to time; every year or even 2-3 times a year for important assortments which record frequent fluctuations in price, and for unimportant ones, once in 2-3 years. Formation of such schedules requires great care. The system is applicable in cases of unforeseen distress, for inferior lots, assortments which can not be sold by auction or tenders and to overcome tendency among traders to keep prices of forest produce low.

References

1. A.K. Jain.Forest. Economics of India.
2. A.S. Guleria Production. Consumption and Trade of Forest Products in India
3. A. Sivarama Prasad. Agricultural Marketing in India-
4. Arnold. J.E.M (1995): Poverty & Conservation. Society and Non-Timber Forest Products in Tropical Asia. Ed. Fox J. Occasional paper No. 19, East West Centre; Honolulu, Hawaii USA.
5. Brown. T.C. (1984): The Concept of Value in Resource Allocation. Land Economic. Pp 231-46.
6. Charlie, S. and Sheona S. (2004): The Importance of Non-Timber Forest Products in Rural Livelihood Security and as Safety Nets: A Review of Evidence From South Africa. In: South Africa Journal of Science 100 Nov/Dec 2004. Pg 58-664.

7. Cooks, M.L. and Wiersum K.F. (2003): The Significance of Plant Diversity to Rural Household in The Eastern Cape Province of South Strica. Forest Trees Livelihood 13 Pg 39-58.

8. Costanza, R., and C. Folke (1997): Valuing Ecosystem Services with Efficiency, Fairness and Sustainability as Goals. Island Press Washington D.C. USA. Pg 49-68.

9. D.N. Tewari. Marketing and Trade of Forest Produce (Practical Book).

10. Emery, M. (1998): Seeing, Gathering, Managing Gathering Special Forest Products and Public Land Management. In Proc, Special Forest Product: Working Together in a changing World. Western Forestry & Conservation Assoc. Portland Oregon Pg 31.

11. Food and Agricultural Organization of the United Nations FAO (1989): Women in Community Forestry in Unasylva Vol. 36 No. 46 April. Rome. pp. 5-7.

12. Food and Agricultural Organization of the United Nations FAO (1990): The Major Significance of "Minor Forest Product. The Local Use and Value of Forest in the West. African Humid Forest Zone. Community Forestry Note 6 Rome.

13. Food and Agricultural Organization of the United Nations FAO (1992): Forest, Trees and food Rome. pp. 2-4 Food and Agricultural Organization of the United Nation FAO (1995): Valuing Forest: Context, Issues and Guidelines, by Gregersen H.M. Arnold J.E.M, Lindgren A.L & Contreras - Hernosilla. FAO Forestry Paper No 127, Rome.

14. Foster, Steven (1995): Forest Pharmacy: Medicinal Plants in American Forest. Forest History Society. Durham NC pg 57.

15. Gbadebo J.O and U. Gloria (1999): The Non-Wood Forest Products of Nigeria. A report produced as out put of the ec-fao partnership programme (1998-2000) project gcp/int/679/ec

16. Hammett, A.L. and J.L. Chamberlain (1998): Sustainable Use of Non-Traditional Forest Product. Alternative Forest Based Income Opportunities. In: Natural Resources Income Opportunities on Private Land Conference. April 5-7th, 1998. Hagerstown, Maryland Ed. Jonathan, S.K. Pg 141-147.

17. K.K. Dewett and J. D. Varma. Elementary Economic Theory

18. K.K. Dewette. Modern Economic Theory

19. Kotler, Philip, 2000, 'Marketing Management- Analysis, Planning and Control', Prentice Hall of India Private Ltd, New Delhi.

20. M.M. Pant.Forest. Economics and Valuation

21. Michael S.G. (1995): Economic Valuation of the Multiple Use of Forest: The Case of Bwindi Impenetrable National Park, Uganda. University of Edinburgh, U.K (M.Sc) dissertation).

22. Murphy, I.K, Bhat P.R., Ravindranah, N.H and R. Sukumar (2005): Financial Valuation of Non-Timber Forest Product Flows in Uttara Kannada District, Western Ghats, Karnataka. In: Current Science, Vol.88, No.10, 25 May, 2005. Pg 1573-1579.

23. New York Times, (1996): From Necessity, New Forest Industry rises. Sunday 24th March. National Report Section, Front page.United Nations (1995): Non-wood News. Writer Food & Agricultural Organisations Rome, Italy.

24. Okafor, J.C.; Omoradion, F.I. and Amaja (1994): Non-Timber Forest Products (Nigeria): Consultancy Paper prepared by the Tropical Forest Action Programme (TFAP) Forest Management, Evaluation and Co-ordination Units (FORMECU) and Federal Department of Forestry (FDF) Abuja, Nigeria. P. 8.

25. Peterson Borin, 1997, 'Marketing- A Contemporary Introduction', John Wiley and Sons, Inc., New York.

26. Ramasamy, V.S, 1998, 'Marketing Management in Indian Environment', Macmillan India Ltd., New Delhi.

27. Rosenberg, Larry. J, 1997, 'Marketing', Prentice Hall Inc., Englewood Cliffs, New York.

28. S.C. Jain. Principles and Practice of Agriculture Marketing and Prices

29. S.S. Achraya and N. L. Agrawal Agricultural Marketing in India

30. Stanton, William.J, 1998, 'Fundamentals of Marketing', Mc Graw Hill Kogakusha Ltd., New Delhi.

31. Star Steven, H, 1997, 'Problems in Marketing', McGraw-Hill Books Company, New York.

❑❑❑

Chapter 14

Model Questions Bank

Choose the Correct Answer for the Following

1. NOVOD Board, Gurgaon is mainly connected with the conducting research on ________
   a) Timber trees   b) Fodder trees
   c) TBOs   d) Pulp and paper
2. Protection of Plant Varieties and Farmers' Right Act ________
   a) 2001   b) 2000
   c) 2002   d) 2004
3. The word "market" comes from the Latin word "marcatus" which means ________
   a) Merchandise   b) Trade
   c) A place   d) All of these
4. Selling function is also referred as ________
   a) Creative function   b) Distribution function
   c) Both   d) None
5. India enacted the Biodiversity Act to ensure maintenance, sustenance and development of its biodiversity in the year ________
   a) 2002   b) 2001
   c) 2003   d) 2000
6. The widening of the market helps in increasing the demand on a continuous basis and there by guarantees a ____________ to the producer
   a) Higher income   b) Lower income
   c) Loss in income   d) None of these

7. The cost involved in moving the product from the point of production to the point of consumption is known as ________

   a) Fixed cost   b) Marketing cost

   c) Market margin   d) Price spread

8. The transportation of forest produces from one place to another place added by the rate, road or water, where it can be consumed or stored is called as ________

   a) Form utility   b) Time utility

   c) Place utility   d) Possession utility

9. New patent laws were made after the independence in the form of the Indian Patent Act in ________

   a) 1970   b) 1980

   c) 1960   d) 1975

10. The most suitable mode of transportation for heavy and bulky commodities to cover long distance quickly in all weather conditions which is very cheap is ________

    a) Water transport   b) Air transport

    c) Rail transport   d) None

11. The best example for an organization which provides facilities for the exchange of commodities is ________

    a) Super market   b) Bombay Stock Exchange

    c) Asian market   d) Indian market

12. The Headquarter of TRIFED is at ________

    a) New Delhi   b) Mumbai

    c) Chennai   d) Hyderabad

13. Any goods or material produced for sale in the market is referred as ________

    a) Demand   b) Commodity

    c) Supply   d) Market

14. AGMARK is situated in ________

    a) Mumbai   b) Nagpur

    c) Hyderabad   d) New Delhi

15. These markets are the biggest markets from the area or coverage point of view ________

    a) International markets   b) Terminal markets

    c) Capital markets   d) All of these

16. Very commonly used methods of sale in India ________

    a) Tender   b) Auction

    c) Both   d) None

17. The industry or industries dependent on agriculture for the supply of raw materials ________

    a) Cotton industry   b) Silk industry

    c) Sugar industry   d) All of these

18. Market which deals with the goods and raw materials, such as plywood, furniture, timber, bamboo and other minor forest produce is known as __________

    a) Capital market   b) Commodity market

    c) Retail market   d) Terminal market

19. The head quarter of WTO is located in ________

    a) Geneva   b) New York

    c) Nairobi   d) None

20. Agar wood (wood oil) is commercially extracted from this tree species ________

    a) Courapita gynensis   b) Aquillaria agallocha

    c) Cedrus deodar   d) Santalum album

21. The Government of India launched a scheme for the establishment of National Grid of Rural Godowns (NGRG) in ________

    a) 1997   b) 1979

    c) 1989   d) 1999

22. TRIPS is related to ________

    a) Tariff reduction   b) Rights of protection

    c) Copy rights   d) None

23. The market in which the products are perishable in nature, prevails only for a day or few hours is called as ________

a) Short period market b) Long period market

c) Periodic market d) Secular market

24. The difference between the price paid by the consumer and the price received by the producer for an equivalent commodity is known as ________

a) Market margin b) Market cost

c) Price spread d) Total cost

25. The primary functions of marketing mainly consists of ________

a) Assembling b) Procurement

c) Processing d) All of these

26. International Tropical Timber Organization (ITTO) was established in the year ________

a) 1986 b) 1996

c) 1976 d) 1968

27. The headquarter of International Tropical Timber Organization (ITTO) is situated in ________

a) USA b) Germany

c) Japan d) Thailand

28. GATT signed in 1947 was replaced by the________ in 1995.

a) ITTO b) WTO

c) ISI d) UNCTAD

29. The quantity of the produce which can be made available to the nonfarm population of the country and residual left with the farmers after meeting his family consumption, farm requirements, social and religions payments is called as ________

a) Marketable surplus b) Total Production

c) Total Consumption d) None

30. GATT is related to the following ________

a) Trade b) Tariffs

c) Both a & b d) Topical Timber Organization

31. It is estimated that the demand for timber is likely to grow from 58 million cubic metres in 2005 to ________ million cubic metres in 2020.

a) 253 b) 153

c) 353 d) 351

32. The supply of wood is projected to increase from 29 million cubic metres in 2000 to ______ million cubic metres in 2020.

a) 60 b) 160

c) 260 d) 16

33. The productivity of timber in India is ________

a) 1.70 m^3/ha/year b) 1.60 m^3/ha/year

c) 2.7 m^3/ha/year d) 0.7 m^3/ha/year

34. The average productivity of timber in the world is ___________

a) 4.1 m^3/ha/year b) 2.1 m^3/ha/year

c) 3.1 m^3/ha/year d) None

35. Spice Board was established in Cochin in the year ________

a) 1987 b) 1978

c) 1997 d) None

36. Indian Standard Institution (ISI) established in 1947 was re-named in 1987 as ________ which is located in New Delhi.

a) Indian Statistical Institute (ISI)

b) Bureau of Indian Standard (BIS)

c) AGMARK

d) None

37. The common method/s of selling forest produce is/are by _____

a) Sale to the highest bidder b) By tender

c) Both a & b d) None

38. The method of selling forest produce which quite is popular and fair though not the best method in getting maximum returns is ________

a) Sealed tender b) Open tender

c) Both a & b d) None

39. This system of selling forest produce is applicable in cases of unforeseen distress, for inferior lots, assortments which cannot be sold by auction or tenders and to overcome tendency among traders to keep prices of forest produce low ________

a) Sealed tender

b) Open tender

c) Both a & b

d) Sale by Royalty or Fixed Tariff

40. MS = Total Production (P) – Total family requirement (C), where "MS" means ________

a) Marketable surplus b) Marketed surplus

c) Both a & b d) None

41. The World Trade Organization (WTO) officially commenced on ____________, replacing the General Agreement on Tariffs and Trade (GATT).

a) 1st Jan, 1995 b) 1st January, 1996

c) 1st January, 1985 d) 1st January, 1975

42. WTO's present Director-General is ________

a) Arthur Daunkel b) Pascal Lamy

c) Roberto Azevêdo d) Mike Moore,

43. The present total number of member countries of WTO as on 2nd March, 2013 is ________

a) 149 b) 139

c) 129 d) 159

44. A firm dealing with forestry products, processing of horticultural products, cloth milling, selling and repairs of electronic equipments, manufacturer of vanaspati and a chain of retail outlets, is an example for the following type of market integration ________

a) Horizontal Integration

b) Vertical Integration

c) Conglomeration

d) Ownership/Contract Integration

45. When a firm performs more than one activity (Whole selling, Transportation, Harvesting, Saw milling, etc.) in the sequence of marketing process, then it is represented by the following type of market integration _______
    a) Horizontal Integration
    b) Vertical Integration
    c) Conglomeration
    d) Ownership/Contract Integration
46. This type of market integration occurs, when a firm or agencies gains control of others firms or agencies performing similar marketing functions at the same level in the marketing sequence _______
    a) Horizontal Integration
    b) Vertical Integration
    c) Conglomeration
    d) Ownership/Contract Integration
47. A process of the integration or expansion of firms by consolidating additional marketing functions and activities under a single management is commonly known as _______
    a) Market structure
    b) Marketing function
    c) Market efficiency
    d) Market Integration
48. The difference between the price paid by the consumer and the price received by the producer for an equivalent commodity is known as _______
    a) Price spread
    b) Marketing cost
    c) Market margin
    d) All of these
49. These middlemen are not regular buyers or sellers but they are specialized in risk taking, as they buy at low price and sell in the off season when price are high _______
    a) Facilitative Middlemen
    b) Agent Middlemen
    c) Merchant Middlemen
    d) Speculative Middleman
50. In the following route, the forest commodities generally move from producer to consumers through intermediaries _______
    a) Direct marketing channel
    b) Indirect marketing channel
    c) Marketing channel
    d) All of these

51. The process of determining the monetary values of forest business transactions is called ________

a) Forest appraisal b) Forest stumpage
c) Both a & b d) None of these

52. The World Intellectual Property Organization was created in the year ________

a) 1967 b) 1947
c) 2007 d) 1987

53. The World Intellectual Property Organization day is observed annually on ________

a) April 26 b) March 21
c) June 5 d) May 1

54. The Dunkel proposals culminated into the final act on ________

a) Dec 15, 1993 b) Dec 15, 1988
c) Dec 15, 1999 d) Dec 15, 2000

55. The ratio of market output (satisfaction) to marketing input (cost of resources) is called ________

a) Marketing Integration b) Vertical Integration
c) Horizontal Integration d) Marketing efficiency

56. According to FAO estimate in 1999, the global production of total round wood was about ________

a) 3335 million m^3 b) 6299 million m^3
c) 8233 million m^3 d) 1144 million m^3

Q. State True or False

1. The WTO was started in the year 1995.
2. In India, there are three agencies to take care of extraction and disposal of forest products.
3. Price denotes the sum paid for a specified quantity and quality of any good or service.
4. Commodity is any goods or material produced for sale in the market.
5. A single producer or sellers controls the entire market is monopoly.

6. Average revenue curve is known as Demand curve.
7. The number of firms in pure or absolute monopoly is many.
8. The demand for many of the forest products is derived demand.
9. Perfect competition is a wider term than the pure competition.
10. The Geneva is headquarter of international treaties.
11. Market is a place or building where commodities are bought and sold.
12. Market is not a social institution.
13. When large number of sellers deal with heterogeneous and differentiated form of a commodity is called monopolistic competition.
14. Mashakhores are big wholesalers or small retailers

    (***Meaning of Mashakhores*:** This is a local term used for big retailers or small wholesalers dealing in fruits and vegetables.)
15. Transportation helps to widening of markets.
16. In phar system of open auction one bid is given for all the lots.
17. Itinerant traders directly purchase the produce from the cultivators.
18. Wholesalers are closest to consumers in marketing channels.
19. Processor is a facilitative middlemen
20. Vertical integration occurs when a firm performs only one activity in the sequence of the marketing process.
21. Average revenue curve is known as demand curve.
22. The number of firms in pure or absolute monopoly is one.
23. The demand for many of the forest products is composite demand.
24. Demand denotes the sum paid for a specified quantity and quality of any good or service.
25. Demand is any goods or materials produced for sale
26. Secular markets are of a permanent nature.
27. In perfect markets, there are a small number of buyers or sellers.
28. In capital markets, bonds, shares and securities are transacted.
29. Risk bearing facilitative function is the accepting of the possibility of loss in the marketing of the product.

30. The retailer wholesaler sells the commodity to retailers and other wholesalers but does not sell in significant amount to ultimate consumers.
31. All forest sales in the forest timber depot must be covered by proper bills, receipts and export challans and the sold timber marked with sale hammer.
32. In the tender sale the prospective buyers indicate their tender rates which they are prepared to pay.
33. Marketing channels are routes through which forest products move from producer to consumers.
34. A reduction in the cost for the same level of satisfaction or an increase in the satisfaction at a given cost will result in improvement in marketing efficiency.
35. Horizontal and vertical integration of market occurs, when a firm performs more than one activity in the sequence of the marketing process.
36. The Malaysia is a headquarter of international treaties.
37. Supply denotes the sum paid for a specified quantity and quality of any good or service.
38. Demand is any goods or materials produced for sale in the market.
39. A few producer or sellers controls the entire market is monopoly.
40. Average revenue curve is known as supply curve.
41. The number of firms in pure or absolute monopoly is many.
42. Perfect competition is a smaller term than the pure competition.
43. Quantity offered for sale in given point of time is known as demand.
44. Ability and willingness to purchase in given point of time is known as supply.
45. WTO is established mainly to facilitate social well fare in the member countries.
46. WTO is outcome of Hong Kong round.
47. Indian market is mixed market economy.

Q. Fill in the Blanks

1. ____________ is an activity, where buyers and sellers meet each other.
2. _______________ markets are located generally in district headquarters.
3. _______________ is market situation in which there is only *"one seller"* of a commodity.
4. Marketing includes all the activities involved in the creation of __________, ____________, __________and ____________ utility.
5. The word 'market' comes from the *Latin* word _____________ which means merchandise or trade or place, where business is conducted.
6. ______________ means maximization of profit by minimizing the cost of production.
7. ___________ means ability and willingness for purchase of a commodity in given point of time.
8. WTO established on ____________
9. The transportation of forest produces from one place to another place added by the rate, road or water, where it can be consumed or stored is called as ____________ utility.
10. Mention the types of imperfect markets based on the situations and the degree of imperfect. a.__________b._________c. ___________d.___________.
11. In ______________ markets, bonds, shares and securities are transacted.
12. The WTO was commenced in the year______
13. A market in which buyers and sellers are drawn from the whole world is ____________ market.
14. The World Intellectual Property Organization Day is observed annually on _________
15. The sum paid for a specified quantity and quality of any goods or services ________________

16. According to theory of cost, the cost of product or commodity is affected by ______________

17. Markets which are located near seashore and are meant mainly for the import/export of goods are known as ____________ markets.

18. Regional markets are the type of markets comes under the classification based on ___________

19. ______________ are those individuals or business concerns that specialize the performing the various marketing functions involved in the purchase and sale of goods as they are moved from producers to consumers.

20. The earnest money deposit is usually ____________percent of the contract value.

21. _____________ is a sale in which articles are sold to the highest bidder.

22. _____________is a type of system of sale of forest products, under this government gets a fixed amount sale proceeds for a lot of known quantity of produce.

23. ______________________ is the profit earned or received by those engaged in marketing.

24. The economic contribution of NTFPs exceeds ____________ percent of the total value of forest based exports from India.

25. In India, the current fuel wood consumption is ______________million m^3 (FAO, 2009).

26. ______________ refers to that part of man's wealth which is used in producing further wealth.

27. A market in which there are more than two but still a few sellers of a commodity is termed as __________________ market.

28. The primary functions of marketing mainly consists of a.________________ b. ___________ c. ________________ .

29. The quantity of the produce which can be made available to the nonfarm population of the country and residual left with the farmers after meeting his family consumption, farm requirements, social and religions payments is called as_______________.

30. In this situation ________________, a large number of sellers deal in heterogeneous and differentiated form of a commodity.
31. ________________markets are the biggest markets from the area or coverage point of view.
32. Any goods or material produced for sale in the market is referred as________________.
33. Market which deals with the goods and raw materials, such as plywood, furniture, timber, bamboo and other minor forest produce is known as ________________.
34. The market, in which the products are perishable in nature, prevails only for a day or few hours is called as ____________ market.
35. Marketable Surplus = P – C,

    Where P =______________ C = ________________.
36. The most suitable mode of transportation for heavy and bulky commodities to cover long distance quickly in all weather conditions which is very cheap is ________________.
37. The utility which is created through the impartation of "Informative advertisement" is known as ______________ utility.
38. Mention the different approaches to the Study of Marketing a. ______________ b. ____________ c.______________ d. ______________
39. Marketing Functions as classified by Kahl's and Uhl's a.______________ b.________________c. ______________
40. ________________ Middlemen (type) are specialized in risk taking where they buy the products at low price and sell them in the off-season, when prices are hiked.
41. Dynamics of Market Structure in which the market structure determines the market________________and ______________.
42. A market integration in which a combination of agencies or activities which are not directly related to each other may operate under a unified management be termed as________________.
43. The cost involved in moving the product from the point of production to the point of consumption is known as __________________.

44. Very commonly used methods of sale of timber and Non Timber forest products in India are _____________ and __________.

45. When a firm performs more than one activity (Wholeselling, Transportation, Harvesting, Saw milling, etc.) in the sequence of marketing process, then it is represented by the ____________ type of market integration.

46. ITTO was established in the year ____________.

47. GATT signed in 1947 was replaced by the _______________in the year_______________.

48. _________________type of market integration occurs, when a firm or agencies gains control of others firms or agencies performing similar marketing functions at the same level in the marketing sequence.

49. It is estimated that the demand for timber is likely to grow from 58 million cubic metres in 2005 to ____________million cubic metres in 2020.

50. The supply of wood is projected to increase from 29 million cubic metres in 2000 to ____________ million cubic metres in 2020.

51. The productivity of timber in India and the world are ______________ and ____________ respectively.

52. Indian Standard Institution (ISI) established in 1947 was re-named in 1987 as _____________ which is located in New Delhi.

53. The method of selling forest produce which is quite popular and fair though not the best method in getting maximum returns is ____________________________

54. WTO's present Director-General is ____________________

55. A firm dealing with forestry products, processing of horticultural products, cloth milling, selling and repairs of electronic equipments, manufacturer of vanspati and a chain of retail outlets, is an example for ___________________type of market integration.

56. The ratio of market output (satisfaction) to marketing input (cost of resources) is known as ___________________________.

57. A process of the integration or expansion of firms by consolidating additional marketing functions and activities under a single management is commonly known as __________________.

58. The difference between the price paid by the consumer and the price received by the producer for an equivalent commodity is known as ____________________.

59. The World Intellectual Property Organization was created in the year ____________ and is observed annually on ____________ this date.

60. The word "market" comes from the Latin word "marcatus" which means __________

61. Gradation of the produce according to quality specification is called as __________(Standardization).

62. Existence of goods, buyers, sellers and demarcation of area are the main ____________ of market (components)

63. Minimum Support Price (MSP) is announced every year for the selected MFPs with the technical support from ________ (TRIFED)

64. In market the __________ can take information or guideline as top which types of forest produce are to be grown, at what extent and quantity sold at a particular time. (producer)

65. In case of sale by __________, price for produce is mutually decided by seller and buyer. (private bargain)

66. The headquarter of National Horticultural Mission (NHB) is at __________ (Gurgaon)

67. TRIFED continued to market tribal products through the network of its retail outlets, namely____________

68. In India (according to FAO, 2009), the current fuel wood consumption is ______ million m^3

69. India's current forest and tree cover is estimated to be __________million ha.

70. The economic contribution of NTFPs exceeds ________ per cent of the total value of forest based exports from India.

71. National Bank for Agriculture and Rural Development (NABARD) is an apex development bank established in the year ______________ in India having headquarters based in ____________

Q. Match the Following

Set I

Part A	Part B
1. Kotler	a) Conversion of teak log into furniture
2. Capital market	b) Import and export of goods
3. Commodity Market	c) Share market
4. Time utility	d) Market as an area for potential exchanges
5. Acharya and Agarwal	e) Timber Depots
6. Form utility	f) Large number of buyers and sellers
7. Perfect market	g) Minor forest produce such as plywood
8. Possession Utility	h) Agricultural Marketing in India
9. N.D. Tiwari	i) Fish from cold storage

Set II

Part A	Part B
1. Form utility	a) Marketing and Trade of Forest produce
2. Capital market	b) Import and export of goods
3. Perfect market	c) Share market
4. Time utility	d) Market as an area for potential exchanges
5. Sea Board Market	e) Timber Depots
6. Kotler	f) Fish from cold storage
7. Commodity Market	g) Minor forest produce such as plywood
8. Possession Utility	h) Agricultural Marketing in India
9. N.D. Tiwari	i) Large number of buyers and sellers
10. Acharya and Agarwal	j) Conversion of teak log into furniture

Set III

Part A	Part B
1. Form utility	a) Tea and coffee by different companies
2. Capital market	b) Import and export of goods
3. Market integration	c) Share market
4. Time utility	d) Advertisement on *Meswak* tooth paste
5. Sea Board Market	e) Timber Depot
6. Commodity Market	f) Amla and tamarind in off-season
7. Knowledge utility	g) Minor forest produce, such as plywood
8. Possession Utility	h) Different air lines operating in our country
9. Oligopoly Market	i) Expansion of firm
10. Monopolistic Competition	j) Conversion of teak log into furniture

Set IV

Part A	Part B
1. Perfect market	a) Exchange of goods
2. Demand forecast	b) Taste
3. Market size	c) Payment at a fixed interval
4. IPR's	d) Money economy
5. Wide market	e) Product
6. Demand	f) Retail market
7. Modern economy	g) WIPO
8. Quantitative	h) Expert opinion
9. Qualitative	i) Delphi method
10. Barter	j) Homogeneous product

Set V

Part A	Part B
1. Location	a) Periodic markets
2. Area coverage	b) Forward markets
3. Time span	c) Primary wholesale markets
4. Volume of transaction	d) Regulated markets
5. Nature of transaction	e) Rural markets
6. Number of commodities	f) National markets
7. Degree of competition	g) Producing markets
8. Govt. intervention	h) Retail markets
9. Population served	i) Perfect markets
10. Stage of Marketing	j) General markets

Set VI

Part A	Part B
1. Capital recovery	a) Advance interest
2. Interest	b) Payment at a fixed interval
3. Demand	c) Rent
4. Modern economy	d) Turnover
5. Barter	e) Exchange of goods
6. Market	f) Homogeneous product
7. Local capital	g) Restricted investment
8. Discount	h) Money economy
9. Royalty sale	i) Taste
10. Perfect market	j) Buyers and sellers

Set VII Part A	Part B
1. GATT	a) Business
2. Interest	b) Payment at a fixed interval
3. Demand	c) Rent
4. Modern economy	d) 1948
5. Barter	e) Exchange of goods
6. WTO	f) Homogeneous product
7. Local capital	g) Restricted investment
8. Trade	h) Money economy
9. Royalty sale	i) 1995
10. Perfect market	j) Buyers and sellers

Q. Expand the Following Abbreviations

1. **AGMARK**- Symbol of Agricultural Marketing on graded products, Nagpur (1953)
2. **APEDA** –Agricultural Processed Food Product & Export Development Agency, New Delhi (1986)
3. **COSAMB** – Council of State Agriculture Marketing Board (1988)
4. **DMI** – Director of Marketing & Inspection, Faridabad (1935)
5. **FCI** – Food Corporation of India, New Delhi (1964)
6. **FDCM** – Forest Development Corporation of Maharashtra Limited, Nagpur (1974)
7. **GATA** - Gold Anti-Trust Action Committee
8. **GATT** - General Agreement on Tariffs and Trade
9. **IMF** - International Monetary Fund (The *International Monetary Fund* (*IMF*) is an international organization headquartered in Washington, D.C., in the United States, of 188 countries)
10. **IPO** – Initial Public Offering (NSE)
11. **ITTO** - International Tropical Timber Organization, Yokohama, Japan
12. **KIAM** – Karnataka Institute of Agricultural Marketing, Mysore.
13. **MFPTDFS** – Minor Forest Products Trading & Development Federations (1992)

14. **MPEDA** - Marine Products Exports Development Authority
15. **MSAMB** - Maharashtra State Agricultural Marketing Board, Pune (1984)
16. **MSCTDC** - Maharashtra State Co-operative Tribal Development Corporation, Nashik (1972)
17. **NABARD** - National Bank for Agricultural and Rural Development
18. **NAFED** - National Agricultural Co-operative Marketing Federation of India.
19. **NCDC** - National Co-operative Development Corporation New Delhi (1976)
20. **NDDB** - National Dairy Development Board, Anand, Gujarat.
21. **NHB** - National Horticulture Board (1984) - Gurgaon.
22. **NIAM** - National Institute of Agricultural Marketing, Jaipur (1988)
23. **NMPB** - National Medicinal Plant Board, New Delhi (2000)
24. **NOVOD** - National Oil seeds and Vegetable Oils Development Board, Gurgaon
25. **STDC** - State Tribal Development Corporation, Mumbai (1972)
26. **STDCCS** - State Tribal Development Co-operative Corporations (1992)
27. **TANFED** - Tamil Nadu Co-operative Marketing Federation Ltd.
28. **TDC** - Tribal Development Corporation, New Delhi (1972)
29. **TMFI** - Tribal Marketing Federation of India
30. **TNCSC** - Tamil Nadu Civil Supplies Corporation Limited (Private Company, 1972)
31. **TRIFED** - Tribal Co-operative Marketing Development Federation of India Limited, New Delhi (1987),
32. **TRIMS** - Trade-Related Investment Measures
33. **TRIPS** - Trade Related Intellectual Property Rights
34. **TRTI** - Tribal Research and Training Institute, Pune (1962)
35. **UNCTAD** - United Nations Conference on Trade and Development

Q. Define the Followingin one Sentence only

1. Trade
2. Market structure
3. Marketing efficiency
4. Marketing integration
5. Regular Market
6. Primary Market
7. Marketing
8. Marketing function
9. Marketable surplus
10. Sea Board Market
11. Marketing channel
12. Price spread
13. Marketing cost
14. Market margin
15. Components of market
16. Periodic Market
17. IPRs
18. Monopoly Market
19. Monopolistic Competition
20. Patent
21. International trade
22. Speculative Middlemen
23. Demand forecasting
24. Copyrights
25. Trademarks
26. WTO
27. GATT
28. ITTO
29. Conglomeration
30. Lump sum sale
31. Tender
32. Auction
33. Bidding
34. Duopoly
35. Mixed economy
36. Trade off
37. Trade name
38. Free economy
39. Trade acceptance
40. Elasticity
41. Internal trade

Q III. Differentiate the Following

1. Perfect market Vs Imperfect markets
2. Monopoly market Vs Duopoly market
3. Direct marketing channel Vs Indirect marketing channel
4. Wholesale market Vs Retail market
5. Short period market Vs Long period market
6. Commodity market Vs Capital market
7. Marketing cost Vs Market margin
8. Horizontal market integration Vs Vertical market integration
9. WTO Vs ITTO
10. Technical marketing Efficiency Vs Pricing marketing Efficiency
11. Marketable surplus Vs Marketed surplus

Q. Answer the Following

1. Give the Kohl's and Uhl's classification of marketing function.
2. Write the marketing channel for any four commercially extracted and marketed forest produce.

3. Define the different types of approaches to study of marketing function.
4. Explain the different types of creation of utilities of the product by market.
5. Write the various dimensions of market
6. Define marketing efficiency and explain the types in brief.
7. Differentiate between the marketing cost and market margin
8. Explain the perfect and imperfect markets.
9. Write about TRIFED and list the objectives of TRIFED
10. Write the role of Government Agencies in Marketing of Forest Produce.
11. Write the advantages and disadvantages of International Trade.
12. Define market structure and explain the components of market structure.
13. Define market integration. Explain the different types market integration.
14. Expand WTO and GATT. Mention the objectives and provisions and disadvantages of GATT.
15. What do you mean by IPR? Explain in brief.
16. Write a note on Economic Valuation of Non-Timber Forest Product and its classification of forest values.
17. What is Demand forecasting? Write the classification of Demand forecasting methods/techniques.
18. Write a note on International Trade.
19. Write a note on ITTO.

Q. Answer the Following

1. Explain the scope and Importance of Marketing
2. Explain the various systems and methods of sale of forest produce/products
3. Write the meaning and structure of market. Explain the classification of market on the basis of location, area/coverage,

time span, nature of commodity, degree of competition and nature of transaction.

4. What is marketing function? Explain in detail the broad classification of marketing function.
5. Define market. Write the detailed classification of markets based on various dimensions and explain.
6. What are the different kinds approaches to study market? Explain briefly.
7. Which are the common methods of selling forest produce? Explain in detail.
8. Explain the role of government and private agencies in exploitation and marketing of forest produce in India.
9. Explain demand forecasting and its broad classification of methods/ techniques.
10. Explain the structure, functions and decision making process of World Trade Organization.
11. Explain the valuation of timber and non-timber products with its classification of forest values.
12. Explain the Market Integration and its classification in detail.
13. Write in detail about the involvement of different agencies in system of exploitation of forest products in India.
14. What is pure competition? Write the conditions of perfect, imperfect and monopolistic competitions.

Appendices

Appendix I

Current Affairs on NTFPs / MFPs

Cabinet has decided on minimum support price (MSP) for 12 minor forest produces for 100 million tribals.

Govt has introduced minimum support price (MSP) mechanism for 12 minor forest produces (MFPs) or non-timber forest produce (NTFP). **These 12 MFPs include :**

1. Lac,	2. Chironji
3. Wild Honey	4. Karanj Seed
5. Mohua Seed	6. Sal Seed
7. Sal Leaf	8. Tamarind
9. Gum Kariya	10. Myrobalan
11. Tendu	12. Bamboo.

The tribal welfare scheme is aimed at providing a safety net for forest-dwellers who depend on minor forest produces for household income and for daily food requirement. According to the proposal, the tribal affairs ministry will put in place a fair price mechanism under Tribal Cooperative Marketing Development Federation of India Limited (TRIFED), the marketing arm of the ministry.

It would fix MSP or a remunerative and fair price for the **12 MFPs**. If the price of the produce gathered by the tribal falls below this price, state's designated agencies would be alerted to procure the MFP. The Centre would share the losses with the state in a 75:25 ratio. The government has ear-marked almost 100 crore for the scheme.

The states covered are: **Andhra Pradesh, Chhattisgarh, Gujarat, Himachal Pradesh, Jharkhand, Madhya Pradesh, Maharashtra, Odisha and Rajasthan.**

TRIFED would put in place a pricing cell, which will draw members from all nine tribal-dominated Schedule V area states. The states would provide the list of MFPs to their cooperative agencies. These MFPs would not be covered under this mechanism and instead the Centre would introduce another MFP for the state and fix its price.

This will not disrupt the already-existent mechanism. If, say tamarind, is already being handled by state agency in Maharashtra, then Govt. would not fix a price for it centrally. Govt. will identify another MFP for Maharashtra. The idea is to provide a fair price to forest gatherers for as many products as possible.

Appendix II

Industries/Firms and Potential Employers of Forestry Graduates in India

S.No.	Name of the Firm/ Industry and Address with contact details
1.	ITC Bhadrachalam Paper & Paper Board Ltd. Khammam, Andhra Pradesh ITC Bhadrachalam Paper & Paper Board Ltd. Khammam District Andhra Pradesh. Registered Office: ITC LIMITED, 37 J. L. Nehru Road, Kolkata - 700071, India. Ph: +91-33-22889371 Website www.itcpspd.com
2.	West Coast paper Mills Ltd., Dandeli, Uttar Kannada, Karnataka West Coast Paper Mills Ltd., Shopping Centre, Bangur Nagar, Dandeli, Dist-Uttara Kannada, Pin -581 325, Karnataka-581325. Phone:+91 82842 31391
3.	Mysore Paper Mills Ltd., Bhadravati, Shimoga District of , Karnataka The Mysore Paper Mills Limited, Bhadravati, Shimoga District of Karnataka. Tel : 080– 22262334, 22354496 , 22266979
4.	Ballarpur Industries Ltd., Yamunanagar, Haryana, Ballarpur Industries Limited - Manufacturer of Paper & Paper Made Products, Printing Paper, Tissue Paper, Copier Paper & Colour Paper from Yamunanagar, India. ... Industries Limited Sushil Atri+91-9812302567. +91-1732-292171. Address: Unit Shree Gopal, Yamuna Nagar, Yamunanagar - 135001, Haryana, India.
5.	Harihar Polyfibres Ltd., Harihar, Davengere, Karnataka, Contact Address, # C 15/4, GRASIM Staff Colony Kumarapatnam P.O. – 581 123. Ranebennur Tq ,Haveri Dist ,KARNATAKA, INDIA. [M/s Grasim Industries Limited, (Aditya Birla Group) and M/S Harihar Polyfibers]

6. Andhra Pradesh Paper Mills Ltd. East Godavari, Andhra Pradesh Division Address: Andhra Pradesh Paper Mills Ltd Unit: Rajahmundry East Godavari Dist. Rajahmundry, AP-533105. Phone : +91-883-2471 831 / 2471837. Email: appmcorp@andhrapaper.com

7. Hindustan Paper Corporation, Morigaon, Cachar, Assam Asst. Public Information Officer, Cachar Paper Mill (Unit), Dist. Morigaon, Assam Phone: (03678) 245900. Fax: (03678) 254143. E-mail: dkb@hindpaper.in

8. Kitply Industries, Tinsukiya, Assam, TINSUKIA Rungagora Road Tinsukia - 786125 (Assam) Ph: 0374-2330838/7530. Fax: 0374-2337530, Email: guwahati@kitply.com

9. Orient Paper Industries, Mahendragarh, Faridabad, Haryana PRINCIPAL OFFICE9/1, R. N. Mukherjee Road, Kolkata, West Bengal, PIN - 700 001, Phone:- (033) 30573700 / 30410900, Fax:- (033) 2243 0490, E-mail: info@orientpaperindia.com, REGISTERED OFFICE Unit - VIII, Plot No. 7 Bhoinagar Bhubaneswar, Odisha-751 012 Tele. (0674) 2396930/2392947, Fax: (0674) 2396364 E-mail: paper@opilbbsr.com

10. Hindustan Newsprint Ltd., Kottayam, Kerala, Hindustan Newsprint Limited, Newsprint Nagar P.O - 686 616, Kottayam District, Kerala, India. Phone: +91 4829 256211 to 256221, Fax: +91 4829 251911.

11. Travencore Reyons, Ernakulam, Kerala, Registered address is 11 55 RAYON PURAM P OPERUMBAVOOR , ERNAKULAM ... Address 2. City, ERNAKULAM. State, Kerala. Country, INDIA. Pin-683543.

12. Western India Plywood Pvt. Ltd. Kannur, Kerala, Address: Baliapatam, Kannur Town , Kerala-670010, India, Phone:+91 497 277 8151

13. Grasim Industries Ltd. Ujjain, Raipur, Mandsaur, Gwalior, Birlagram, Nagda-456 331, Madhya Pradesh, India, Tel: 91-07366-246760/ 246766, Fax: 91-07366-244114/246024, Email: shares@adity abirla.com, Website: www.adityabirla.com

14. Orient Paper Industries Ltd., Shahdol, Madhya Pradesh, Orient Paper & Industries Limited ... Fax:- (033) 2243 0490.... ORIENT PAPER Mills. P.O.:- Amlai Paper Mills Dist.:- Shahdol Madhya Pradesh, PIN - 484 117. Tel No.:- (07652) 286275 / 286277. Fax:-(07652)286274 .E-mail:info@orientpaperindia.com, E-mail: unit_amlai@orient paperindia.com

15. J. K. Industries, Raigada, Orrisa, Head Office: JK Paper Limited, Nehru House 3rd Floor, 4 Bahadurshah Zafar Marg, New Delhi –110002. Phone No.: 91-11-33001112, 33001132. Fax No.: 91- 11 – 2371 2680. Work Pffice: JK Paper Mills, Jaykaypur, Distt. Rayagada-765017, Orissa – 765 017, India. Phone : 91-6856-233303, 233770, 233171, 233550, 233087, 234077-79 91-6856-222238

16. Venus plywood Pvt. Ltd., V. Raowali, Pathankot Road, Jalandhar, Punjab, Village Raowali, Pathankot Road, Jalandhar City, Jalandhar - 144001, Ph No: +(91)-181-2603756, +(91)-9872819191

17. Star Paper Mills, Ltd., Saharanpur, Uttara Pradesh, Address: Paper Mill Rd, Saharanpur, Uttar Pradesh-247001, India, Phone:+91 132 671 4101

18. WIMCO match, Barreily, Uttara Pradesh, Address: NEAR- AMARPALI MALL, C.B. GUNJ, Bareilly - 243502, Uttar Pradesh, India Phone No: +91-581-2560252, Contact Person: Mr.Sandeep Sharma (Commercial Manager), Mobile: +918938808807.

19. Century paper and Pulp Ltd., Lalkunwa, Haldawani, Nainital, Uttaranchal, Address: Guru Gobindsingh Marg, Lalkuan, Lucknow, Uttar Pradesh-226001, India, Phone:+91 5945 268 046

20. Kitply Industries, Calcutta, West Bengal, Address: 119, 4th Floor, White House, 'a' Block, Park Street, Park Street, Kolkata, West Bengal-700016, India, Phone:+91 33 2229 3344

21. Pudumjee Pulp and Paper Mills Ltd., Jatia Chambers, 60, Dr. V.B. Gandhi Marg, Mumbai -400 023, Maharashtra, Maharashtra Pudumjee Pulp & Paper Mills Ltd. ... 60, Dr. V.B. Gandhi Marg, Fort.-400023 Mumbai, India. Tel: View phone number +91 22 30213333; Fax: +91 22 22658316;

Appendix III

Important Wood Based Industries in India

Andhra Pradesh	ITC Bhadrachalam Paper & Paper Board Ltd. Khamman, A. P.
	Andhra Pradesh Paper Mills Ltd. East Godavari, A.P
	Ryalseema Paper Mills, Ryalseema, A.P.
Assam	Hindustan Paper Corporation, Morigaon, Cachar, Assam
	Kitply Industries, Tinsukiya, Assam
	Jayshree Tea & Industries, Sibsagar, Kachhar, Jorhat, Assam
	National Plywood Industries Pvt. Ltd., Tinsukia, Kamrup, Assam
	WIMCO Match Ltd., Goalpara, Assam
Haryana	Ballarpur Industries Ltd., Yamunanagar, Haryana
	Orient Paper Industries, Mahendragarh, Faridabad, Haryana
Karnataka	Mysore Paper Mills Ltd., Shimoga, Karnataka

	West Coast paper Mills Ltd., Dandeli, Uttar Kannada
	Harihar Polyfibres Ltd., Harihar, Davengere, Karnataka
Kerala	Grasim Industries Ltd., Kozhikode, Kerala
	Hindustan Newsprint Ltd., Kottayam, Kerala
	Travencore Reyons, Ernakulam, Kerala
	Western India Plywood Pvt. Ltd. Kannur, Kerala
Madhya Pradesh	Grasim Industries Ltd. Ujjain, Raipur, Mandsaur, Gwalior
	Orient Paper Industries Ltd., Shahdol, MP
Odisha	J. K. Industries, Raigada, Odisha
	Orient Paper Mills Ltd., Sambalpur. Odisha
	Ballarpur Paper Industries, Cuttak, Odisha
	Mangalam timber Products Ltd. Navrangpur, Odisha
Punjab	Nuchem Ltd., Meeting Point, SCO 487-88, Sector 35-C, Chandigarh
	Northern India Plywood Manufacturers Association (NIPMA)
	Venus plywood Pvt. Ltd., V. Raowali, Pathankot Road, Jalandhar
Uttar Pradesh	Star Paper Mills, Ltd., Saharanpur, U.P.
	WIMCO match, Barreily, U.P.
Uttaranchal	Century paper and Pulp Ltd., Lalkunwa, Haldawani, Nainital, Uttaranchal
	WIMCO Seedlings Pvt. Ltd., Bagwala, Udhamsingh Nagar, Uttaranchal
Tamil Nadu	Tamilnadu Newsprint, Tiruchirapalli, Tamil Nadu
West Bengal	Kitply Industries, Kolkata, West Bengal
Maharashtra	Pudumjee Pulp and Paper Mills Ltd., Jatia Chambers, 60, Dr. V.B. Gandhi Marg, Mumbai -400 023

Appendix IV

Government and Private Agencies in Marketing of Forest Produce

1. **NOVOD** - National Oilseeds and Vegetable Oils Development Board, Gurgaon, Haryana.
2. **ISI** - Indian Standard Institution (1947). It is re-named as Bureau of Indian Standard (BIS), New Delhi (1987)
3. **NHB** - National Horticulture Board (1984), Gurgaon.
4. **Spice Board** - Cochin (1987)

5. **COSAMB** - Council of State Agriculture Marketing Board (1988)
6. **NCDC** - National Co-operative Development Corporation New Delhi. (1976)
7. **FCI** - Food Corporation of India, New Delhi (1964)
8. **TDC** - Tribal Development Corporation, New Delhi (1972)
9. **FDCM** - Forest Development Corporation of Maharashtra Limited, Nagpur (1974)
10. **TMFI** - Tribals Mission Foundation International, Philippines (1985)
11. **TRIFED** - Tribal Co-operative Marketing Development Federation of India Limited, New Delhi (1987),
12. **STDC** - State Tribal Development Corporation, Mumbai (1972)
13. **MFPTDFS** - Minor Forest Product (Trading and Development) Federations (1992)
14. **STDCCS** - State Tribal Development Cooperative Corporations (1992)
15. **NIAM** - National Institute of Agricultural Marketing, Jaipur (1988)
16. **NAFED** - National Agricultural Co-operative Marketing Federation of India
17. **NMPB** - National Medicinal Plant Board, New Delhi (2000)
18. **APEDA** -Agricultural Processed Products and Export Development Agency, New Delhi (1986)
19. **TRTI** - Tribal Research and Training Institute, Pune (1962)
20. **MSCTDC**- Maharashtra State Co-operative Tribal Development Corporation, Nashik (1972)
21. **MSAMB**-Maharashtra State Agricultural Marketing Board, Pune (1984)
22. **AGMARK**- Agricultural Marketing, Nagpur (1953) (Symbol of Agril. Marketing on graded products).
23. **NABARD** - National Bank for Agriculture and Rural Development.

24. **KIAM** – Karnataka Institute of Agricultural Marketing, Mysore.
25. **NDDB** – National Dairy Development Board, Anand, Gujarat.
26. **TANFED** – Tamil Nadu Co-operative Marketing Federation Ltd (Popularly known as TANFED)
27. **MPEDA-** Marine Products Exports Development Authority.
28. **OFDC** - The Odisha Forest Development Corporation (OFDC) trades timber in round and sawn forms, in different dimensions, from several depots. Round timbers are sold monthly from each depot, through general auction.

Appendix V

Indian Council of Forestry Research and Education (ICFRE)

भारतीय वानिकी अनुसंधान एवं शिक्षा परिषद्

The Indian Council of Forestry Research and Education (ICFRE) is an autonomous organisation or governmental agency under the Ministry of Environment and Forests, Government of India. Headquartered in Dehradun, its functions are to conduct forestry research; transfer the technologies developed to the states of India and other user agencies; and to impart forestry education. The council has 9 research institutes and 4 advanced centres to cater to the research needs of different bio-geographical regions. These are located at Dehradun, Shimla, Ranchi, Jorhat, Jabalpur, Jodhpur, Bangalore, Coimbatore, Allahabad, Chhindwara, Aizawl, Hyderabad and Agartala.

Type	**Autonomous Organisation**
Established	**1986**
Parent institution	**Ministry of Environment and Forests (India)**
President	**Maanas**
Director	**Maanas**
Location	**P.O. New Forest, Dehradun, Uttarakhand, India 248006** **30.345192°N 78.002193°ECoordinates: 30.345192°N 78.002193°E**
Campus	**Urban**
Acronym	**ICFRE (भा.वा.अ.शि.प.)**
Website	**www.icfre.org//**

History

ICFRE is the largest organisation responsible for forestry research in India. ICFRE was created in 1986, under the Ministry of Environment and Forests (India), to direct and manage research and education in forestry sector in India. ICFRE is headed by a Director General with headquarters at Dehradun. ICFRE became an autonomous council under the Ministry in 1991.

Mandate

The mandate of the ICFRE is to organise, direct and manage research and education in the forestry sector, including in cooperation with FORTIP (UNDP/FAO Regional Forest Tree Improvement Project), UNDP and World Bank on economically important species. ICFRE established a National Bureau of Forest Genetic Resources (NBFGR).

Research perspective

- Conservation, protection, regeneration, rehabilitation and sustainable development of natural forest ecosystems.
- Revegetation of barren, waste, marginal and mined lands.
- Research on tree improvement.
- Enhancing productivity of wood and non-wood forest produce per unit of area per unit time by application of scientific and technological methods.
- Research on improved utilisation, recovery and processing of forest produce for value addition and employment generation.
- Ecological rehabilitation of all fragile ecosystems, such as mountains, mangroves, deserts, etc.
- Socio-economic and policy research for developing strategies towards attracting people's participation in forest management.

Research Institutes

Institute and their locations, sorted alphabetically					
Name	**Acronym**	**Established**	**City**	**Jurisdiction**	**Website**
Arid Forest Research Institute (AFRI)	AFRI	1988	Jodhpur	Rajasthan, Gujarat, Dadra and Nagar Haveli	afri.res.in
Forest Research Institute (FRI)	FRI	1906	Dehradun	Punjab, Haryana, Chandigarh, Delhi, U.P., Uttarakhand	fri.icfre.gov.in
Himalayan Forest Research Institute (HFRI)	HFRI	1977	Shimla	Himachal Pradesh, Jammu and Kashmir	hfri.icfre.gov.in
Institute of Forest Biodiversity (IFB)	IFB	2012	Hyderabad	Telangana, Maharashtra	frc.icfre.gov.in
Institute of Forest Genetics and Tree Breeding (IFGTB)	IFGTB	1988	Coimbatore	T.N., Kerala, A & Nicobar, Lakshadweep, Pondicherry	ifgtb.icfre.gov.in#/
Institute of Forest Productivity (IFP)	IFP	1993	Ranchi	Bihar, Jharkhand, Sikkim, West Bengal	ifpranchi.co.in
Institute of Wood Science and Technology (IWST)	IWST	1938	Bangalore	Karnataka, Telangana, Andhra Pradesh, Goa	iwst.icfre.gov.in#/
Rain Forest Research Institute (RFRI)	RFRI	1988	Jorhat	North-east India	rfri.icfre.gov.in
Tropical Forest Research Institute (TFRI)	TFRI	1988	Jabalpur	M.P., Chhattisgarh, Maharashtra, Odisha	tfri.icfre.gov.in

Advanced research centres

Institute and their locations, sorted alphabetically					
Name	**Acronym**	**Established**	**City**	**Jurisdiction**	**Website**
Advanced Research Centre for Bamboo and Rattan (a unit of RFRI)	ARCBR	2004	Aizawl	North-east India	www.icfre.org
Centre for Forestry Research and Human Resource Development (satellite centre of TFRI)	CFRHRD	1995	Chhindwara	M.P., Chhattisgarh, Maharashtra, Odisha	www.icfre.org
Centre for Social Forestry and Eco-Rehabilitation (a centre of ICFRE)	CSFER	1992	Allahabad	Eastern U.P., North Bihar, Vindhya Range	www.icfre.org
Centre for Forest Based Livelihood and Extension[2][14]	CFLE	2013	Agartala	Tripura	tripurainfo
Centre for Urban Forestry Research (a centre of AFRI)	CUFR	(Planned)	Gandhinagar	Gujarat	

Appendix VI

List of Agricultural Universities in India

State Agricultural Universities / Central University

1. Acharya NG Ranga Agricultural Univ., Rajendranagar, Hyderabad-500030, A.P
2. Anand Agricultural University, Anand-388110, Gujarat
3. Assam Agricultural University, Jorhat-785013, Assam
4. Bidhan Chandra Krishi Viswavidyalaya, P.O Krishi Viswavidyalaya, Mohanpur, Nadia-741252, West Bengal
5. Birsa Agricultural University, Kanke, Ranchi- 834006, Jharkhand
6. Central Agricultural University, Imphal -795004, Manipur
7. Chandra Shekar Azad Univ. of Agriculture & Technology, Kanpur- 208002, U.P
8. Chaudhary Charan Singh Haryana Agricultural University, Hissar-125004,Haryana
9. Chaudhary Sarwan Kumar Himachal Pradesh Krishi Vishwavidyalaya, Palampur, Kangra- 176062, Himachal Pradesh
10. Dr Balasaheb Sawant Konkan Krishi Vidyapeeth, Dapoli, Ratnagiri-415712, Maharashtra
11. Dr Panjabrao Deshmukh Krishi Vidyapeeth, Krishi Nagar, Akola-444104, Maharashtra
12. Dr Yashwant Singh Parmar Univ. of Horticulture & Forestry, Solan, Nauni - 173230, Himachal Pradesh
13. Govind Ballabh Pant University of Agriculture & Technology, Pantnagar, Udhamsingh Nagar-263145, Uttarakhand
14. Guru Angad Dev University of Veterinary and Animal Sciences, Ludhiana-141004, Punjab
15. Indira Gandhi Krishi Vishwavidyalaya, Krishak Nagar, Raipur-492006, Chhattisgarh
16. Jawaharlal Nehru Krishi Vishwavidyalaya, Krishi Nagar, Jabalpur- 482004, M.P.
17. Junagadh Agriculture University, Moti Bagh, Agril. Campus, Junagadh-362001, Gujarat

18. Karnataka Veterinary Animal and Fisheries Science University, P.B. No. 6, Nandinagar, Bidar-585401, Karnataka
19. Kerala Agricultural University, P.O Vellanikkara, Thrissur-680656, Kerala
20. Maharana Pratap Univ. of Agriculture & Technology, Udaipur-313001, Rajasthan
21. Maharashtra Animal Science & Fishery University, Nagpur, Maharashtra
22. Mahatma Phule Krishi Vidyapeeth, Rahuri-413722, Maharashtra
23. Marathwada Agricultural University, Parbhani -431402, Maharashtra
24. Narendra Deva University of Agriculture & Technology, Kumarganj, Faizabad- 224229, Uttar Pradesh
25. Navsari Agricultural University, Vijalpore, Navsari-396450, Gujarat
26. Orissa Univ. of Agriculture & Technology, Siripur, Bhubaneswar-751003, Odisha
27. Punjab Agricultural University, Ludhiana -141004, Punjab
28. Rajasthan AgriculturalUniversity, Bikaner -334006, Rajasthan
29. Rajendra Agricultural University, Pusa, Samastipur-848125, Bihar
30. Sardar Vallabh Bhai Patel Univ of Agriculture & Technology, Modipuram, Meerut-250110, Uttar Pradesh
31. Sardarkrushinagar-Dantiwada Agricultural University, Sardarkrushinagar, Dantiwada, Banaskantha-385506, Gujarat
32. Sher-E-Kashmir Univ. of Agricultural Sciences & Technology, Railway Road, Jammu- 180012 (J&K)
33. Sher-E-Kashmir Univ. of Agricultural Sciences & Technology, Shalimar, Srinagar- 191121, (J&K)
34. Sri Venkateswara Veterinary University, Tirupati, Chittoor-517502, A.P.
35. Tamil Nadu Agricultural University, Coimbatore-641003, Tamil Nadu
36. Tamil Nadu Veterinary & Animal Sciences University, Madhavaram Milk Colony, Chennai- 600051, Tamil Nadu
37. University of Agricultural Sciences, Dharwad, Karnataka

38. University of Agricultural Sciences, Bengaluru-560065, Karnataka
39. UP Pandit Deen Dayal Upadhayay Pashu Chikitsa Vigyan Vishwavidyalaya Evam Go Anusandhan Sansthan, Mathura-281001, Uttar Pradesh
40. Uttar Banga Krishi Vishwavidyalaya, P.O. Pundibari, Distt. Cooch Behar-736165, West Bengal
41. West Bengal University of Animal & Fishery Sciences, 68 KB Sarani, Kolkata-700037, West Bengal
42. University of Horticultural Sciences, Venkataramnagudem, West Godavari, A.P.
43. Rajmata VRS Agricultural University, Gwalior-474002, Madhya Pradesh
44. University of Horticultural Sciences, Navanagar, Bagalkot-587101, Karnataka
45. University of Agricultural Sciences, Raichur-584102, Karnataka

Deemed-to-be Universities

1. Indian Agricultural Research Institute, Pusa-110012, New Delhi
2. Indian Veterinary Research Institute, Izatnagar, Bareilly-243122, Uttar Pradesh
3. National Dairy Research Institute, Karnal-132001, Haryana
4. Central Institute of Fisheries Education, Mumbai-400061, Maharashtra
5. Allahabad Agricultural Institute, Allahabad-211007, Uttar Pradesh

Central Universities with Agriculture Faculty

1. Banaras Hindu University, Varanasi, U.P.
2. Aligarh Muslim University, Aligarh, U.P.
3. Vishwa Bharati, Shantiniketan, West Bengal
4. Nagaland University, Medizipherma, Nagaland

❑❑❑